THE SPY
WHO PAINTED
THE QUEEN
THE SECRET CASE AGAINST
PHILIP DE LÁSZLÓ

D1502649

THE SPY WHO PAINTED THE QUEEN

THE SECRET CASE AGAINST PHILIP DE LÁSZLÓ

PHIL TOMASELLI

Front cover illustration © Shutterstock

First published 2015

The History Press
The Mill, Brimscombe Port
Stroud, Gloucestershire, GL5 2QG
www.thehistorypress.co.uk

© Phil Tomaselli, 2015

The right of Phil Tomaselli to be identified as the Author
of this work has been asserted in accordance with the
Copyright, Designs and Patents Act 1988.

British Library Cataloguing in Publication Data.
A catalogue record for this book is available from the British Library.

ISBN 978 0 7509 6053 3

Typesetting and origination by The History Press
Printed and bound in Great Britain by TJ International Ltd.

CONTENTS

INTRODUCTION

THE CENTENARY PUBLICATION of MI5's official history *The Defence of the Realm: The Authorised History of MI5* by Christopher Andrew may have given some people the idea that everything there is to say about the organisation's history has already been said. In fact, it devotes only fifty-six pages to the First World War and, though there are a few other splendid books on their work in that period (and some terrible ones), much remains to be discovered and written.

Though the spies uncovered, arrested, charged and sentenced as a result of MI5's work are pretty well covered in the literature (though I doubt many could name all sixty-five), one little-explored area is the progressive restrictions imposed upon, and eventual internment of, the 226 men of hostile origin or association (other than alien enemies) interned specifically because of MI5's direct action. These were in addition to the thousands of German, Austro-Hungarian and Turkish men of military age or considered a security threat, some of whom had lived in Britain for years, who were interned and, in the case of most of the older men, eventually deported. Considering much of MI5's work before August 1914 centred on identifying the potential threat posed by German and Austrian immigrants (including identifying them through illegal use of the 1911 census and the running of agents into their communities), this is a surprising omission, though a lot of hard work is required to find material, much of which appears to have been destroyed after the war. Philip De László, having been born in Hungary and naturalised as British (albeit after the start of the war), comes into the first category, though I doubt he could be considered typical of it. In his case there seems to have been concrete intelligence of hostile acts and hostile intent. His MI5 file, if it survived the organisation's steady weeding of old material, has not been released, but sufficient information remains in files of related government agencies to reconstruct the bones of it.

This is not a nice story. De László comes across as, at least initially, an extremely likeable chap. Raised from poverty on the back of his own talents, a romantic who pursued his wife in the face of all kinds of objections from her posh relatives, a family man, a patriot (though for quite which side may be debated), he seems to have done his best for both sides of his family in the course of an international conflict that slaughtered millions and brought down empires. The standard biographies (one of which he helped write) show him as a confused and decent enough man, his patriotic instincts naturally divided, who made honest mistakes and was condemned for his decent endeavours by vindictive British authorities who were determined to get him to pay for errors it was easy enough to make. This is how he presented himself to the world for twenty years following his success before the Denaturalisation Committee in 1919 (the nearest he came to a trial), and he seems to have been successful. Unfortunately for him, and for his biographers, there was an unexamined and ticking time-bomb lurking in the Home Office and Treasury solicitors' papers at The National

Archives (TNA) in Kew. They present the other case – that seen by MI5, Special Branch and the Secret Intelligence Service – that he was a deliberate and cynical agent of an enemy power acting as both a source of important high-level intelligence and a peace propaganda source, spreading ill-will towards Britain's allies and undermining the morale of his important clients among Britain's elite. This is the evidence that will be presented here. Though I have made up my mind on the subject, others may come to a different conclusion, but it is a story that requires telling nonetheless.

There's a contemporary resonance in this case, which illustrates the difficulty the intelligence agencies had, and still have, in pursuing people they suspect of being a danger to security. The evidence presented to the public at the Denaturalisation Committee in 1919 appeared – and indeed was – slight. If anything, it made the authorities look petty and spiteful, though that could be said of other cases, as we shall see. But there was more serious evidence, provided by the French secret service from a secret agent allegedly working at the heart of a German and Austrian intelligence-gathering network based in Switzerland, that never appeared in public. Even if it was examined secretly by the Denaturalisation Committee, it was dismissed without any serious consideration (they took fifteen minutes to clear De László on almost all counts, though the committee that reviewed his internment did treat it more seriously). Without the permission of the French, who would not want such a valuable and sensitive source compromised by exposure in court, MI5, the Police and the Home Office could not use this evidence to prosecute De László and there was no mechanism for secret courts in which he could be tried.

The decision by British judges, a couple of years ago, to release secret American documents relating to Binyam Mohamed's treatment at Guantanamo Bay – and the resulting American threat to downgrade intelligence sharing with the UK – highlighted the delicate relationship between secret services and the information they exchange. The necessity to conceal the origin of secret intelligence has, on occasion, caused similar problems in other terrorist trials. The De László files at The National Archives show this has long been a problem – and that in the case of the prominent society artist, the reluctance of MI5 to reveal its sources worked to his advantage.

Acknowledgements

I ORIGINALLY DISCOVERED that MI5 had been investigating De László when I stumbled upon a cartoon in one of the MI5 cartoon books (produced for internal consumption only, but which occasionally come on the market) that my good friend Dr Nick Hiley showed me. I owe Nick a considerable debt of gratitude for his assistance, advice and support for this book as for several of my others. Many thanks are also due to Julian Putkowski, who gave me his copy of the other MI5 cartoon book gratis, carried out some splendid research on various members of MI5 staff which he shared with me and found much information on the mysterious Frederic Decseny. Thomas Boghardt, on hearing I intended to mention the Baron von Horst case, kindly sent me a copy of an article he'd written on it, which backed up my own researches and conclusions. Edwin Ruis provided background information on the German intelligence service in Holland. Professor Rick Spence, with whom I've worked on a number of projects, kindly helped me to unpick the relationships between the various banks in the USA and checked the Bureau of Investigation files for me.

The Metropolitan Police kindly searched their archives and confirmed they no longer hold any files on de László. Staff at the Foreign Office and the US National Archives and Research Administration (NARA) searched their records for information on Frederic Decseny for me. Staff at the Home Office also searched their records for anything on Desceny and for the missing sub-file 113 in De László's naturalisation file, but were unable to locate anything. Peter Day scoured online newspaper archives for me in search of Desceny. Kim Thomason offered advice on the tying (and possible means of opening) of diplomatic bags. As usual the staff at The National Archives provided their excellent service and assistance, and the staff at North Swindon Library have tracked down various obscure reference books for me. The publishers of *Who's Who* provided me with information on De László's early entries in their book.

I've referred to the Security Service as MI5 throughout the book, though purists will realise that before April 1916 they were known, within the War Office and to the police and other authorities, as MO5g, the counter-espionage section of the larger MO5 which, in its turn, formed part of the Directorate of Special Intelligence at the War Office. The Directorate also dealt with Press Censorship (MO7), Cable Censorship (MO8) and Postal Censorship (MO9) as well as liaison with the foreign secret service (the Secret Intelligence Service, sometimes now called MI6), examination of enemy ciphers, arms traffic and collation of intelligence. Since the name MI5 was assumed in 1916 (when the other MO sections became MI7, MI8 and MI9) the existence of this secret service department has become generally acknowledged and referred to as MI5 by the general public. I've stuck with the common parlance for the ease of the reader. It's also worth noting that, when referring back to themselves after 1916, they used MI5 rather than trying to explain the changes.

1

SPIES AND
RUMOURS OF SPIES

FEBRUARY 1915 WAS the seventh month of a war that had been supposed by many to have been over by the previous Christmas. In London it was cold, but not unseasonably so. In Flanders the original British Expeditionary Force (BEF) had fought the Retreat from Mons, the Battle of the Marne and the First Battle of Ypres, and was horribly exhausted. Only the influx of fresh troops from the garrisons in the empire, Indian troops and battalions of the part-time Territorial Force had allowed them to hold their portion of the trench line that now snaked between the Belgian coast and the Swiss border. At sea the Royal Navy had had successes at the Battle of the Heligoland Bight in August 1914 when British cruisers and destroyers ambushed a German destroyer patrol, sinking three light cruisers and a destroyer, and at Dogger Bank in January 1915 where they sank the armoured cruiser *Blucher*. They'd also skirmished with German Zeppelins and seaplanes after the Royal Naval Air Service's attempt to bomb the Zeppelin shed at Cuxhaven on Christmas Day. But the Navy too had taken some terrible casualties: three old cruisers, *Aboukir, Crecy* and *Hogue* had been sunk, within a couple of hours by one submarine, with the loss of 1,459 lives, and Rear Admiral Christopher Craddock's South Atlantic Squadron had been effectively destroyed at the Battle of Coronel off the coast of Chile on 1 November 1914 (subsequently avenged at the Battle of the Falklands on 8 December).

At home, even the casual observer would notice the new recruits for the army training daily in the local parks and would know of their male relatives who had volunteered or were being pressured daily by the White Feather League who gave white feathers, denoting cowardice, to young men not in uniform. The human cost of the war was known; casualty lists in the newspapers named officers and men who were known to be killed, wounded or missing and covered several columns of newsprint every day. The public was perfectly aware of the price being paid by its soldiers and seamen but there was no rationing and, as yet, no blackout.

There had been other casualties that brought the fact that this was a modern, total war, home to civilians. German cruisers had shelled Great Yarmouth in November, fortunately without causing casualties in the town. They then, much more seriously, bombarded Hartlepool, Scarborough and Whitby on 16 December 1914, killing 137 and wounding 592, most of them civilians. Though there had long been a fear of air raids by the much-vaunted Zeppelin fleet, the first raids had been by German aircraft, dropping bombs into Dover Harbour on 21 December and making an abortive attack on London on Christmas Day. On 19 and 20 January, however, a Zeppelin had crossed the coast near Great Yarmouth and dropped six high explosive and seven incendiary bombs on the town. A sister ship dropped a scattering of small bombs on Norfolk villages and the bulk of its load onto King's Lynn. Four civilians had been killed and sixteen injured. Newspaper correspondents regaled their readers with stories of houses with their doors and windows shattered, of children killed or horribly injured, of miraculous escapes and the composure of the populace under the threat of the airborne menace. If the Germans could carry out these raids with apparent impunity, could they not carry out the threat that had lingered in British minds since Erskine Childers published *The Riddle of the Sands* in 1903, a full-scale invasion of the country backed by a secret army of spies and saboteurs?

Stories of a secret army had been circulating for years. A popular subject for fiction, it made a good living for authors like William Le Queux whose novel *The Invasion of 1910* (published in 1906) told the story of a German invasion supported by 100 spies, concealed among the German expatriate population, who had blown up key railway bridges and telegraph lines. He expanded on the theme in his *Spies of the Kaiser: Plotting the Downfall of England* in 1909, in which a German head agent in London led a group of 5,000 agents throughout the country.

The press took up the fascination with enemy spies and began reporting a series of fantastic stories alleging espionage activity. Some newspapers, with a bit more sense, rubbished the stories, not that it made much difference. The *Western Times* of 22 August 1908 summed up some of the alleged cases:

If an affable foreigner wanders amid the glades of Epping Forest, or takes a photograph of its leafy splendours, he is made the subject of excited letters to the press. The waiters who flock to ... the East Coast resorts during our brief summer cannot beguile their scanty leisure by a little sea fishing without raising, in the fevered imagination of some onlooker, that they are taking soundings. Apprehensive publicists invite us to believe that, at a given signal, the foreign servants who throng some of our hotels will suddenly be revealed as a far more formidable phalanx of warriors than the wooden horse disclosed to the disconcerted vision of the people of Troy.

In the main, however, the press continued to run with the fancies of their readership, and in the *Daily Mail,* when it serialised *The Invasion of 1910,* the route taken by the German invaders was altered to have them march through and terrorise major towns where it was felt the *Mail* wasn't selling well enough. Special maps were printed showing the route so that new readers could be encouraged to buy the paper to read how their town had fared. The paper added 80,000 to its circulation while the story was running. Le Queux's mediocre plots and appalling literary style didn't stop his books selling, or coming to the attention of the War Office where MO5, the small special intelligence section dealing with espionage abroad and counter-intelligence at home, were beginning to pick up a few reports of their own suggesting German espionage was taking place.

MO5 was headed by Major James Edmonds. He was almost as convinced of the German threat as Le Queux, who influenced him heavily, as did a more sober War Office analysis of Germany's success in the Franco-Prussian War of 1870, which showed, in part, it was owed to a highly organised secret service operating in France, to which the French had no response. A ruckus was being made in the press and questions raised in Parliament, including, 'I beg to ask the Secretary of State for War whether he has received any official information or reports from chief constables in the Eastern Counties as to espionage in England by Foreign nations; and, if so, whether he attaches any importance to the information.' For these reasons Prime Minister Herbert Asquith instructed the Committee of Imperial Defence (CID) to consider the dangers from German espionage to British naval ports and, almost incidentally, to look at British information on Germany itself.

The CID eventually recommended the formation of a Secret Service Bureau to carry out espionage at home and abroad. The foreign side went to Captain Mansfield Smith

Cumming RN, who had a broad range of interests in technology, being a motorcar racer, an expert on engines and soon to learn to fly. Since most of the espionage to be done abroad was on behalf of the navy and targeted the German fleet, this is not surprising. Counter-intelligence at home went to 35-year-old Captain Vernon George Waldegrave Kell of the South Staffordshire Regiment, who was a fluent speaker of French, German, Russian and Italian. He had served in China in 1900 as aide de camp, and served on the staff (as special service officer) between 1900 and 1903. During the Boxer Rebellion he took part in the relief of Pekin and also learned Chinese. He had spent two years (1907–09) compiling the history of the Russo-Japanese War for the Imperial Defence Committee. He had also travelled extensively worldwide. Though not called it at the time, this was the origin of the MI5.

Kell assumed responsibility for a former Metropolitan Police Special Branch officer, William Melville, who had been used since 1904 as a kind of War Office private detective, and with his aid, and the assistance of a handful of other officers, began to try and track down enemy spies. Though there were plenty of rumours to be investigated, it was only when one of Kell's officers accidentally overheard two Germans discussing a mysterious letter one of them had received from Germany asking him to supply information, that they got on the trail of actual espionage. From this slender lead, Kell's small organisation was able to track down several German spies who were working for their Naval Intelligence Department, mainly by identifying the addresses they were sending their reports to and having all mail to those addresses stopped and checked by the Post Office. Kell's team established the important principle that its secret methods were rarely revealed, and it waited until a known spy slipped up publicly or was reported as a possible spy by the police or public before it acted and had him or her arrested. Despite its successes against spies, it still had not been able to find the supposed network of saboteurs and this remained a source of worry. Were there still hundreds of German agents out there?

In addition to MI5 as a line of defence against spies, saboteurs and other political malefactors, there was the older Special Branch of the Metropolitan Police, which had been formed in 1883 as the Special Irish Branch, to deal with the spate of Irish republican bombings the country was then suffering from. The Irish problem gradually abated, but 'The Branch' continued in existence, taking over a number of roles relating to state security ranging from the basic checking of the bona fides of aliens within the Metropolitan Police seeking to naturalise as British, to what would now be described as royal and diplomatic protection and keeping an eye on the many foreigners who came to Britain for political reasons. A few Branch officers worked in foreign ports watching passengers to Britain, and there were some based at British ports watching arrivals and departures.

Because of the nature of their work, these officers were usually well-educated and frequently spoke several languages. Herbert Fitch – who once hid in a cupboard to eavesdrop during a Bolshevik Party meeting in London attended by Lenin – spoke French, German and Russian. Naturally, they liaised closely with the MI5 because MI5 officers did not have powers of arrest and preferred to work in secret. The Branch also had the manpower to carry out basic enquiries such as discreet chats with neighbours about individuals and watching railway stations, though the outbreak of war saw it too fully stretched, even though its numbers had been considerably augmented before the war to watch the Suffragette movement. Some men had gone to France with the army as the nucleus of the Intelligence Corps, and other officers were posted full time to the ports, but this still left a nucleus of about 100 experienced officers to carry out 'political' or sensitive investigations.

Once MI5 had decided on the arrest of a suspect, details were passed to Special Branch to carry out the arrest and to take over the case for prosecution, though MI5 officers would frequently appear at the trial as experts 'from a Department of the War Office'. Close liaison between the two departments was essential, and MI5 commended 124 branch officers for their assistance at the end of the war. The Branch carried out its own investigations, but, MI5 later noted, not a single spy was caught by it working on its own; all successful prosecutions for espionage came from information provided by MI5.

Basil Thomson was head of the Metropolitan Police Criminal Investigation Department (CID) and also of Special Branch in his capacity as Assistant Commissioner (Crime) (ACC). These were the days when a well-educated man was assumed to be capable of doing just about anything, and Thomson was a case in point. Born in 1861, son of a Church of England priest who later became Archbishop of York, he'd been educated at Eton and New College, Oxford. Joining the Colonial Service, he served as a magistrate in Fiji and in New Guinea before being invalided back to Britain. He married and then returned to the Pacific where he was prime minister of Tonga for a time. Returning again to Britain, he wrote memoirs of his time in Fiji and Tonga, as well as a novel, while studying Law. He was called to the Bar in 1896 and then became deputy governor of Liverpool Prison, then governor of Dartmoor and Wormwood Scrubs and, between 1908 and 1913, secretary to the Prison Commission. In 1913 he was appointed Assistant Commissioner (Crime) for the Metropolitan Police (this was a time when senior police posts were usually held by men appointed from outside), with an office at Scotland Yard. These were the forces ranged against enemy spies in the event of war.

The outbreak of war came suddenly and unexpectedly, though, of course, the army and navy, as well as MI5, had plans in place to deal with events. The army called up its reserves and the part-time soldiers of the Territorial Force, and set in train sending the BEF to France. The navy had been at the annual Fleet Review in the Solent at the end of July 1914 so it was simply kept on standby as events unfolded and was perfectly ready when war was declared on 4 August.

Acting in part on the advice of MI5 when it came to security matters, the government, through King George V, hastily issued a proclamation commanding his subjects to:

> obey and conform to all instructions and regulations which may be issued by Us or our Admiralty or Army Council, or any Officer of our Navy or Army … and not to hinder or obstruct, but to afford all assistance in their power to, any person acting in accordance with such instructions or regulations …

Within a few days this had crystallised into the Defence of the Realm Act (DORA) that was rushed through Parliament. It gave the military sweeping powers to (among others) commandeer land and buildings and to prepare them for defence or destroy them; it gave them right of access to any building or property whatsoever, to remove people from an area, and to restrict the sale of alcohol. There were explicit restrictions on publication or communication of any information on the armed forces that might be of use to the enemy and bans on photograph-ing, drawing, modelling or possessing plans of fortifications, docks or other installations. There were also bans on tamper-ing or interfering with telephone or telegraph lines or having equipment to tap them, on damaging railways or attempting to injure soldiers guarding them, on possession of dynamite or other explosives, on spreading alarm or disaffection, showing unauthorised lights and on tampering with passes and docu-ments. Anyone committing, attempting to commit or assisting in the commission of these offences would be tried by court martial and liable to a sentence of 'penal servitude for life or any less punishment'. Sweeping powers were granted to 'Competent Military Authorities', defined by the Act as 'any commissioned officer of His Majesty's Naval or Military Forces, not below the rank of commander in the Navy, or Lieutenant Colonel in the Army, appointed by the Admiralty or Army Council, as the case may be, to perform in any place the duties of such an authority'.

DORA was passed simultaneously with the Aliens Restriction Act (again largely inspired by MI5), which imposed draconian restrictions on aliens (foreigners) of all nationalities. It restricted their arrival or departure to one of thirteen named ports and the landing of enemy aliens to only those who had been granted a permit. It also allowed Home Office aliens officers to restrict the landing of any alien and the legal detention of any alien landing without the correct authorisation, prevented them leaving the country without authority and obliged the master of any vessel to report aliens aboard and not allow them to land without the alien officer's permission. Restrictions were also made on aliens resident in Britain. There were immediate restrictions placed upon where they could live – a whole series of areas adjacent to the coast, ports and military establishments becoming areas from which they were banned without permission. All aliens, whether hostile or not, were obliged to register with the Registration Officer (usually a senior police officer) of their district and to inform them of any planned move as well as advising the Registration Officer of their new district and registering their families. They were forbidden to keep firearms, petrol or other inflammable substances, a motor car, motor cycle or aircraft, any signalling apparatus of any kind, any cipher or code or to keep pigeons. A justice of the peace or policeman with the rank of superintendent or higher could sign a warrant authorising a police raid, using force if necessary, upon their premises at any time. Penalties for any breach of the act could not exceed a fine of £100 or a prison sentence of six months, with or without hard labour.

The Aliens Restriction Bill had been presented to the House of Commons by the Home Secretary, Mr Reginald McKenna, on 5 August 1914 when he told the House:

One of the main objects of the Bill is to remove or restrain the movements of undesirable aliens, especially with a view to the removal or detention of spies. Information in the possession of the Government proves that cases of espionage have been frequent in recent years, and many spies have been caught and dealt with by the police. Within the last twenty-four hours no fewer than twenty-one spies, or suspected spies, have been arrested in various places all over the country, chiefly in important military or naval centres, some of them long known to the authorities to be spies.

It's an interesting statement. In later years, especially when budgets were being restricted or there was talk of amalgamating MI5 with one or other of the intelligence services, the great spy round-up of 4 August 1914 would be trotted out to justify MI5's existence. The list of agents arrested has appeared in various forms over the years (usually including men arrested on their own initiative by local police on what appear to be highly suspect grounds), but even the most theoretically significant list, compiled by Professor Christopher Andrew and his researchers for the MI5 official history, can't get round the fact that, of the twenty-two spies listed, only ten were arrested on 4 August and the last wasn't arrested until the 16th. But the story was out; it was in Hansard and in the newspapers, so it must have been true!

The passing of the two pieces of legislation didn't calm the spy scare; in fact the announcement that twenty-one had been rounded up on the first day of the war probably boosted it. In an early debate in the House of Lords, Lord Leith of Fyvie alleged that the law, as it stood, gave the police few powers against aliens 'against whom we have no absolute proof' and also that some eighty-two enemy aliens were at large in Aberdeen, some of whom were 'known' to have been signalling on the coast and others to have been photographing fishing boats. He went on:

> A much more serious item is this. Within a mile-and-a-half of our principal naval wireless station at Aberdeen lives a noted German. He is an ex-captain in the Prussian Army and has been called out, twice. Each time it has been said, 'Never mind; you stay there.' Anyhow he has gone through two wars with honours given to him, and yet he is allowed to reside within a mile-and-a-half of our principal naval wireless station. The Police have no power to go into his house. They have at present two men constantly shadowing him.

The number of alleged spies was legion. Alfred Thielemann was charged with being in possession of photographic apparatus, military maps and other items without a permit. A detective officer described how he'd found a number of photographic negatives of Hull harbour and Liverpool docks as well as permits to photograph the Port of London and the Manchester Ship Canal. The defendant pleaded that he was employed by a German company, the European Lantern Slide Company, which had an office in Newgate Street, London, and that he had been sent from Berlin in April to take photographs for them and had been unable to get back to Germany on the outbreak of war. Remanding him in custody, the magistrate remarked, 'This case may turn out to be one of importance.' It didn't.

A German named William Hark was arrested at the head-quarters of the Royal Engineers' Territorial Regiment whilst dressed in military uniform. He was charged with failing to register but pointed out he'd lived in England for twenty-five years and served as a volunteer soldier for twenty, so he had assumed the law did not apply to him. An officer vouched for his service and character, but he was remanded in custody.

Sergeant Bottcher of the 6th (Territorial Force) Battalion of the Essex Regiment was investigated because:

> while stationed on the East Coast, [he] endeavoured to get his late employer to ask for him to come to London for three days, the said Serjeant associating with the cook at a house the owner of which is a Sin Feiner and the cook of which was in the habit of visiting Germany.

Whatever the result of the investigation, Bottcher went on to serve honourably in the Middle East, ending the war as a company quartermaster sergeant major with the 1914/15 Star, British War Medal, Victory Medal and Territorial Force Efficiency Medal.

A member of a Southsea concert party who was on a ferry from Ventnor was arrested for looking at a naval vessel through a pair of opera glasses, but released after a short detention.

Mrs Lockwood, wife of a former army officer, reported a suspicious German on Primrose Hill whom she had seen walking his dog. When she turned to look at him, she saw 'a pigeon on a level with his head about three yards in front flying away … though she did not actually see the pigeon leave his hand, she considered it must have come from him (and) she noticed a little white paper under the pigeon's wing'. Peter Duhn, aged 28, described as a well-dressed German living in Charlotte Crescent, Regent's Park, had quite correctly registered himself with the police as required, but was charged with not notifying them that he owned a pigeon (though no evidence apart from that of Mrs Lockwood seems to have been presented that he did). He was convicted and sentenced to six months' imprisonment.

It wasn't just the police and MI5 that were deluged with reports. A naval investigator in Devon submitted a report in January 1915 on a house known as 'Snail's Castle' near Totnes, where the owner, a London-based lawyer, Mr Blackwell, had been reported for his suspicious behaviour. He visited the property in the company of a mysterious lady and was reported on one occasion to have taken a car, late at night, to Torcross Sands and to have been left there with no obvious means of going on. An interview with the driver proved that, in fact, he'd been taken to a local hotel. His visits were irregular and, it was said, he always arrived late at night, which had occasioned much gossip. As the investigator noted, 'Mr Blackwell is a married man and the lady who accompanies him to Snail's Castle is not his wife, which may account for something.' It almost certainly accounted for everything.

The military were inevitably caught up in the scare as well. MT1(b), the War Office section that collated and circulated home defence intelligence reports, issued regular updates. These included those of an army officer who had visited the works of the Danish Butter Company at Erith and reported:

I climbed to the roof which is made of concrete 2 ft thick. This roof is flat and dominates the two Railways North and South of the river, the Arsenal, the Purfleet magazines and the whole of the river up to Tilbury on the one side and the Becton Gas Works on the other. There are a considerable number of people employed here, and the majority are Germans, the Manager of the business we learned is a retired German Naval Lieutenant, and we particularly noticed that any of the workpeople who passed us during our Inspection of the Buildings invariably saluted him.

Scores of other buildings, both industrial and domestic, were examined by the police and soldiers who commented on their positions commanding important roads and railways. Other reports detail strange lights seen on the coast, apparently signalling to submarines, though the reports are usually inconclusive. There are reports of strange motor cars in the vicinity of vital points, of strangers buying Scottish islands that might be used as submarine or Zeppelin bases, and mysterious persons asking too many questions.

As far as I can see there is only one genuine case of spying that MT1(b) picked up – that of 'a yacht, the *Sayonara* (which) has been cruising round certain ports on the West Coast of Ireland'. Unfortunately, and unbeknown to the military authorities, this was actually part of a Naval Intelligence and Secret Intelligence Service operation to examine the coast for German submarine bases. Needless to say, it found none.

There were voices that were all too keen to keep the 'spy menace' in the public eye for their own interests. William Le Queux wrote a long article in *The People* on 28 February 1915, headlined 'Hotbeds of Alien Enemies and Spies in the Heart of the Metropolis', alleging the Home Office was turning a blind eye to 'treason mongers and traitors'. It told vivid tales of the authorities allowing 'the scum of Europe' to sit in obscure Soho cafés and restaurants gloating over their 'piratical successes' (the U-Boats) and discussing the coming of the Zeppelins as a signal for thousands of secret agents to combine, presumably in the previously much-vaunted attacks on military and political targets. He described 'a man singing an obscene German song, in which the vilest abuse was levelled against England – our one enemy', with the English being described as 'big heads', 'swine' and 'vermin'. A confidential Special Branch report described Le Queux as a man 'who writes sensational novels on the secret service activities of Germany' and noted that 'Mr Le Queux, in this way advertises himself and his works'. Special Branch was quite right about Le Queux – and, as events were to show, there were others quite happy to jump on the bandwagon of hostility to aliens.

There were suspicions that highly-placed Germans and other enemy aliens, 'some naturalised, some not', were in secret sympathy with Germany and might pose a security risk. An anonymous writer to the letters page in *The Times* advised that the newspaper's correspondence, telephone calls and telegrams be closely monitored, adding in a sinister manner, 'I do not wish to be an alarmist, but I know what I am writing about.'

The Times, commenting on the plethora of reports coming from around the country and the large number of letters it had received from the public, advised, 'The duty of the public is a simple one. It is to report to the police wherever they think there is justification for such a step. A watchful public will form an excellent adjunct to the already hard worked police and the Special Police Force.' With advice such as this, from such an august source, was it surprising that spy fever and fear of foreigners gripped the nation throughout the war?

2

CENSORS, COUNTER-SPIES
AND A SUSPECT

THE OUTBREAK OF war saw the creation of two other, highly effective, defensive and intelligence-gathering organisations. The monitoring of telegrams and letters, as advocated by the anonymous *Times* correspondent, began as soon as the war started. During the Boer War there had been extensive interception of telegrams round the world, and though the organisation responsible for this had been wound up, the necessary machinery still existed to restart it. Cable censorship began immediately, as the War Office had a plan and officers in place to carry out the work. The British had realised at the start of the war that control of information was going to be vital. Their first act of the war was to signal the Post Office cable ship *Alert*, standing by off the German coast, to grapple, cut and reel up the German transatlantic cables, thus forcing the Germans to use neutral cables, which ran through London and could be intercepted. Among the countries that had no cable system of their own was Holland, which was obliged to use the British-controlled lines, as were the other neutral countries in northern Europe. The elimination of key radio transmitters such as the German one in Togoland also helped force the Germans to use neutral cables or their own powerful transmitters in Germany, which could, of course, be picked up by anyone who knew the frequency. Naval Intelligence soon set to work breaking German ciphers, which they managed to do with great success.

During August 1914, censorship was introduced on all post to and from Holland and Scandinavia. Communication with family and friends in enemy countries was not actually banned and censorship rules relating to harmless social communications with alien enemies were simple. Provided they were sent through the normal mail via an intermediary in a neutral country, against whom nothing was suspected, communications were allowed to pass abroad. A note on the subject on De László's file (which has been crossed out) does make the point that, 'This course avoided undue hardship and provided HM Government with a lot of useful information.' The official report on postal censorship states that, gradually, from scraps picked up in individual letters, it was possible to build up a picture of which men were being called up, details of where units were posted, information on troop morale, casualties, details of how German ships in distant waters received supplies, information on new submarines and, from postal censorship sources alone, the writing of a 'Who's Who' of the German Naval Zeppelin Service with biographies of most of its officers. Letters sent through suspect intermediaries were thoroughly scrutinised by the censorship staff and, unless they were clearly utterly harmless, were stopped from going forward.

Business letters and transfers of money were also allowed to pass, provided they were licensed by the Board of Trade or Treasury and sent through an unobjectionable intermediary. The chief postal censor received copies of all licences issued under the Trading with the Enemy legislation so that any correspondence could be checked against the current list of licences.

In August 1917, arrangements were made with Thomas Cook & Sons to act as a bulk intermediary to help poorer people who might otherwise struggle to find an approved neutral, though other approved intermediaries could still be used.

Any letter posted in the usual way (i.e. without going through an approved intermediary and without the relevant authority), within Britain but to an address abroad that hinted at transfers of money to an enemy, were passed to the relevant authorities for action to be taken. Similarly, any letter that mentioned or hinted at communication being sent through the agency of a neutral embassy, consulate or legation should also be passed over, firstly to the Foreign Office, so that they could, if necessary, make representations to the legation to have it stopped, and secondly to any other authority concerned with the breach of the law. As we shall see, due to the volume of mail being checked, some such correspondence was not always identified.

Though the censorship services were by no means perfect, especially early in the war, they did valuable work. They'd helped MI5 to score its first success against visiting German agents when, in August and September 1914, a telegram and letter sent to a suspicious address in Stockholm were identified. The Germans were not aware that their pre-war addresses for receiving spy communications had been compromised, and continued to use them. A Post Office clerk, Malcolm Brodie, a specialist in the clandestine opening of envelopes and in codes and invisible inks who had been seconded to MI5 since July 1913, identified the message in the telegram as a code and, on opening the letter, found a sealed envelope inside addressed to Berlin which, when opened, contained a letter in German giving details of shipping losses and locations of naval vessels. Further letters were intercepted and MI5 realised the sender was going under the name of Inglis and was based in Edinburgh. Edinburgh Police tracked down where he had been staying but in the meantime another intercepted letter revealed he had travelled to Dublin and that the amount and quality of the information he was sending were dangerously improved. The Royal Irish Constabulary traced him to Killarney and arrested him in his hotel there. He turned out to be Carl Hans Lody, a German who had spent time in America and could pose successfully as an American. Despite MI5's objections, he was tried in public at the Old Bailey. Against overwhelming evidence against him, his behaviour in the dock, where he was revealed to be a German officer and not just a 'common spy', won him much admiration. He was, nevertheless, found guilty and sentenced to death. He was shot by firing squad in the Tower of London on 6 November 1914, the first of a dozen to be executed there during the war.

The censorship department continued to keep up its good work. On 16 February 1915, cable censors intercepted a suspect telegram addressed to 'Van Riemsdyk, 8 Orange-Straat, The Hague' which read, 'Please forward amount to László Uteza 28 and wire Lamar postponing journey writing.' The censor had added the note, 'The word Uteza in annexed message is "street" in the Hungarian language, and László is a very usual Hungarian name. This message is clearly for Hungary.' As part of the Austro-Hungarian Empire, with which Britain had been at war since 12 August 1914, this appeared to refer to a breach of the defence regulations on sending money to enemy countries, and the telegram was forwarded to MI5 at its HQ in Watergate House in York Buildings just off the Strand.

Thanks to rapid expansion and the calling up of former intelligence officers, some of whom had served previously in the Boer War, by the beginning of February 1915 MI5 consisted of twenty-three officers (from the army and navy) and officials (the civilian equivalent of officers), and forty-three clerical staff (mostly female, though with a few ex-soldier clerks), orderlies,

chauffeurs, telephone operators, domestics and Boy Scouts and Girl Guides (who acted as internal messengers). Almost all had joined since August 1914, and many were still learning the intricacies of the index card system, the file registry and the procedures for recording and looking up information. In addition, under William Melville, there were two other detectives for making discreet enquiries and three male Post Office employees with expertise in opening envelopes and detecting invisible inks. Melville also controlled three secret agents on behalf of MI5 who infiltrated the alien communities. It wasn't a large organisation, and what resources it had had been extremely stretched since the outbreak of hostilities, with hundreds of reports from the public, police and military coming in weekly, as well as just as many requests for information. The filing system all but collapsed. Though the appointment of a War Office clerk, Miss Steuart, prevented things getting worse, it was only with the February 1915 appointment of Edith Annie Lomax, a former senior secretary in the music publishing industry, that things began to improve once she grabbed the staff by the scruff of the neck and imposed the necessary levels of discipline and rigorous procedures. The message from the censor clearly seemed to indicate an attempt by someone to transmit money to an enemy country and needed following up.

Lacking resources of its own, MI5 relied heavily on the local police to carry out low-level investigations on its behalf, and a request was sent to Bath Police to investigate the sender of the telegram. A few days later they received a report from Inspector Marshfield dated 22 February, which read:

In reply to your letter 11825 (A4) of the 19th instant respecting a telegram sent on the 16th instant by Mr Philip De László of Lansdown Grove Hotel, I beg to inform you that this man is a visitor at the hotel together with his wife. He is a high class

portrait painter and has a permanent address in London. He is a
Hungarian by birth, but became a naturalized British subject on
August 29th 1914. He produced his certificate of naturalization
to the officer who interviewed him. He stated that the telegram
was sent to a friend of his at The Hague for him to send particulars to Hungary respecting his mother who has recently died,
as the message would take a good deal longer by any other route.

MI5 noticed that De László had, apparently, lied about the
telegram's purpose, noting, in a later memo they sent to the
Foreign Trade Department, that he had 'given an explanation
that does not fit in with the wording of the telegram', adding
the comment, 'this discrepancy was noted by us at the time but
we forebore to take further action then as we anticipated that
further proof might be subsequently forthcoming.'

It wasn't to be the only time De László misrepresented the
meaning of the telegram; in the book *Portrait of a Painter* on
which he collaborated with Owen Rutter before his death, it was
claimed that the telegram 'Please forward amount to László
Uteza 28 and wire Lamar postponing journey writing' was a
message to his brother inviting him to a meeting in Amsterdam
following the death of their mother. Hardly so, and he had sat
through that part of the Denaturalisation Committee hearing
which dealt with the matter, so was well aware of the fact.

The name De László, along with variants of it, the subject
and the address of the hotel in Bath, would have been entered
into MI5's card index and cross-referenced with the original
correspondence for ease of 'look up' should any of them come
to attention again.

With more definite information, MI5 could now solidly
identify the sender of the telegram. No doubt he appeared in
their analysis of foreign-born residents from the 1911 census,
where he is the only Philip László, and appears as resident at

3, Palace Gate, West London, aged 42 and of Hungarian nationality, along with his 40-year-old wife Lucy, born in Dublin and
his sons Stephen, aged 6, born in Vienna, and Patrick, 2, born
in London. They also had a cook, four maids, two nurses and a
button boy. This was not a poor household.

A glance at *Who's Who* would have provided some basic information (he first appeared in the book in 1905 as Filip László),
including the fact that he had been made a member of the
Royal Victorian Order in 1910 and had painted Pope Leo XIII
in 1900, the late King Edward VII and other British and foreign
dignitaries. He had also held numerous foreign honours, won
innumerable awards and married into the wealthy Guinness
family. This was a man with connections, and clearly not someone with whom one would tangle without great care. He had
also had an interesting life and was a fascinating man, even
without their suspicions.

Laub Fulop (in Hungarian the surname is quoted first and
Fulop is equivalent to the English name Philip) had been born
on 30 April 1869 in Pest, Roumania (now part of Budapest),
the third child of a poor family. His father, Adolf, was a tailor.
He had two older sisters, then below him another brother
and another sister; three more boys might possibly have died
in infancy, and he had another brother who died in his 30s.
His mother Johanna had been a governess. The family were
Jewish and lived in the Jewish quarter. They spoke German at
home (though Fulop's was always idiosyncratic), but he probably learned Hungarian at school. According to family stories
Fulop was always interested in shapes and colours, and started
drawing at an early age.

Following a difficult education (he was nothing if not opin-
ionated, even as a small child), Fulop left school after being
humiliated by his headmaster at the age of 9. After attending
an exhibition of the great Hungarian artist Mihály Munkácsy,

and being highly impressed by what he saw, he took work as a scenery painter, then as assistant to an architectural sculptor. He left after he was, he claimed, bullied by the other apprentices. He was then apprenticed to Ignac Fischer, a well-known painter of porcelain and majolica, but he left again (after eight months) because of bullying. He had abandoned school and three promising apprenticeships by the age of 12. After a short spell working for a sign painter he was apprenticed to Lipot Strelisky, society photographer, and given the task of hand-tinting photos. At the age of 15, a quick sketch he had made of Count Jeno Zichy led to an introduction to the head of the state-funded School of Decorative Arts, and Zichy allowed him to study there two evenings a week. At 17 he was admitted as a visiting student to the Academy of Arts and won a competition to become a pupil of the artist Karoly Lotz. He took private coaching in mathematics to help him pass the necessary certificate required to enter university, which in turn allowed him to defer national service until the age of 23.

In 1888, he won a state scholarship allowing him to study at the Accademia di Belle Arti in Venice, then at Munich and finally at the Académie Julian in Paris. He then returned to Munich where, in 1892, he met Lucy Guinness, the daughter of Henry Guinness, a banker, of Burton Hall near Dublin. He fell desperately in love and followed her to Paris to press his suit, and the feelings were discovered to be mutual. Though he now had a small reputation as a portrait painter, he was still impoverished, and her family objected to the union. They continued their relationship by post. De László returned to Budapest in 1892 to do his national service, but after only a few weeks he was discharged with varicose veins. In Budapest his talent was recognised by Elek Lippich, secretary of the Fine Arts Department at the Ministry of Education, who supported him and probably secured for him a commission to paint the prime minister,

Sándor Wekerle, which led to De László's first royal commission. It was for two portraits, of Prince Ferdinand of Bulgaria and his consort Princess Marie Louise, for which Ferdinand awarded him the Bulgarian Order of Art and Science. Back in Pest in 1895 he was commissioned to travel to Dresden to copy the only known portrait of Prince Ferenc Rákóczi II, the man who had led the Hungarian struggle for independence from the Hapsburgs in the eighteenth century. While in Dresden he won other important commissions, and on his return to Budapest he began painting members of the old Hungarian noble houses. By 1896 he had an established reputation in his own country and a growing one abroad, and had converted to Christianity. He was starting to earn considerable amounts of money and built a five-storey house that boasted three studios, which he intended for him and Lucy to live in if and when they were allowed to marry.

In 1899 he was awarded the Gold Medal at the Paris Salon for a portrait of Prince Hohenlohe, painted the Emperor Franz Joseph of Austria and won another Gold Medal in Paris in 1900 for a portrait of Pope Leo XIII. In June 1900 he finally married his beloved Lucy at a ceremony in Stillorgan parish church in Dublin and the couple travelled to Budapest to take up residence in his specially-built house. Their first son, Henry, was born there in June 1901.

De László was now in great demand internationally and spent a great deal of time travelling. In 1903 the family moved to Vienna following the death of their second son. In 1907 he was invited to give his first exhibition at the Fine Art Society gallery in Bond Street and then to paint Princess Victoria, King Edward (painted in morning dress for the first time) and Queen Alexandra. Society people flocked to him to have their portraits painted. The family took up residence at 3, Palace Gate, London, close to Kensington Palace and the Royal College of Art, and in the centre of the diplomatic quarter. The family seemed settled, the demand for portraits continued to be strong and paid well and De László professed a long-held admiration for Britain and its institutions. He made many friends amongst his clientele, including Arthur Lee, MP for South Hampshire, Arthur Balfour, former Conservative prime minister and many other members of both Houses of Parliament. He was also invited to royal garden parties. His international commissions still came thick and fast. He painted the American president, Theodore Roosevelt, in 1908 and an official portrait of Kaiser Wilhelm in 1909. In 1910 he was made a Member of the Royal Victorian Order and in 1912 was ennobled by Franz Joseph, Emperor of Austria and King of Hungary. By early 1914, De László was at the height of his powers and all appeared well with the world.

On 24 July 1915, an MI5 official, Mr Robert Nathan, wrote to Mr Moylan at the Home Office requesting, 'May we please see the naturalisation papers of László, the artist (Philip Alexius László de Lombas)? He was granted a certificate of naturalisation on 29/8/14.' This may have been in response (though it seems slightly delayed) to the interception of a postcard dated 18 June from Madame van Riemsdyk in Holland referring to the use of the diplomatic bag to send correspondence to him via the Dutch Legation in London. It may also be linked to a reference in some of the MI5 correspondence, which says, 'Information was subsequently [i.e. after the Bath Police interview] received from a reliable source that De László was sending money from this country to his relatives in Hungary, and steps were accordingly taken to exercise special supervision over his correspondence.' The reliable source was almost certainly the normal censorship which had intercepted a letter dated 3 March 1915 referring to another money transfer. Whichever it was, 'special supervision' meant all post addressed to De László through the ordinary mail was put into the hands of the

Post Office Special Section to be opened and, at the very least, copied before being sent on. Unlike mail from abroad, opened by the Censorship Department, which was opened blatantly and bore a large sticker 'Passed by Censor', this mail was identified at the local sorting office and sent to be opened secretly by a team of highly trained Post Office clerks who could read and speak French and German and who learned Dutch in their own time after war was declared because of the number of letters they had to check written in that language.

This 'Special Section' was closely linked to MI5 and included Malcolm Brodie, who had been involved in the Carl Lody case, and two colleagues, Frederick Bosworth Booth and John Barr Fetherston. They were given honorary military rank and became fully fledged MI5 officers. Their methods remain secret to this day, though the steam kettle was used, as was a long, thin instrument that could be used to roll up a letter very tight, inside a sealed envelope, and then draw it out through a small gap at the top. It's not explained how they got it back in again! These men were experts, and MI5 depended heavily on their expertise. They faced a number of German ploys to prevent or detect tampering with their letters including envelopes stuck together with adhesives that were immune to steam treatment, the placing of special chemicals in an envelope that would change colour if in contact with moisture, the use of wax seals, and the careful and intricate folding and placing of letters within the envelope. Spur-of-the-moment solutions had to be invented, among them the boiling of the notepaper and, on several occasions, the complete reproduction of the correspondence and envelope. As far as they knew, these duplications were never discovered.

During the war, the Special Section officers found themselves having to exercise much greater discretion than previously over whether a particular piece of correspondence should be photographed or copied, or have extracts copied or tested for invisible ink. Their expertise in identifying codes within telegrams resulted in the belated discovery of two German agents, Haicke Marinus Jannsen and Willem Johannes Roos, after a retrospective examination of over 200,000 sent telegram forms, when it was feared that naval intelligence was reaching Germany by this route and being missed by the normal censorship. Roos and Jannsen were shot in the Tower of London. Some highly trustworthy postmasters in the rest of the country were trained in their methods but, as they pointed out in a report:

> To the inexperienced the opening and re-sealing of a letter once demonstrated appear to present little difficulty, but except when dealing with the simplest type of envelope, it is found that the novice's handling betrays itself on close inspection. The expert opener is able to avoid difficulties which the novice does not foresee, he is able to remedy accidents, to remove incriminating traces of his operations, to adapt his methods to the emergency.

London-based suspects such as De László continued to be monitored by the three Special Section officers. The normal Censorship Department was not aware of this arrangement, or of any special checks to be made on De László's correspondence until July 1916.

Robert Nathan, the MI5 official leading the investigation at this stage, had joined the organisation on 4 November 1914. A 48-year-old Indian civil servant, he had returned home on sick leave and been sent to serve as an interpreter to the Indian troops at the front, then joined MI5, where his previous experience in counter-terrorism work was most useful. Educated at St Peter's College, Cambridge, he was a qualified barrister. Joining the Indian civil service in 1888, he had held a number of important posts, including private secretary to the Viceroy.

Whilst commissioner of the Dacca Division, Eastern Bengal, in 1907, he had, working pretty much on his own, uncovered the Anusinal Samitia nationalist terrorist organisation in Bengal. He was later officiating chief secretary to the governor of Eastern Bengal and Assam and president of Dacca and Patna University committees. He held the Companion of the Order of the Indian Empire (awarded in 1903) and the Companion of the Star of India (1911). Though there are occasional allegations that MI5 was anti-semitic, Nathan was Jewish, as were at least two other prominent MI5 officers of the period, and their religion seems not to have held him, or them, back.

In the summer of 1915, Nathan was working as an officer in MI5's A2 section, responsible for the 'Investigation of cases of suspected espionage, sedition or treachery in the United Kingdom without the Metropolitan or City of London Police Areas'. Presumably this was A2's case, because the original transgression had been committed in Bath. Alongside Nathan in A2 were fellow Indian civil servant Percy Marsh, a former assistant magistrate and adviser to the governor of the United Provinces, and Captain Hugh Steuart Gladstone, son of a former governor of the Bank of England, ornithologist, landowner, county councillor, former Boer War intelligence officer and amateur cartoonist.

It was clear from De László's naturalisation papers, when Nathan examined them, that he was a man who had to be treated cautiously. As in all naturalisation applications, he'd been obliged to provide statements from men who knew him well, testifying to his good character. Rather than the usual neighbours and local businessmen one generally finds in such applications, De László produced statements by The Right Honourable Arthur James Balfour, former Conservative prime minister, The Right Honourable Baron Devonport, former Liberal MP for Devonport, chairman of the Port of London Authority and wealthy businessman, Arthur Lee, MP for South

Hampshire, and De László's brother-in-law, the banker Henry Guinness. It was quite possibly because of the involvement of these senior and influential people that it was decided merely to keep a postal check on him.

Every piece of mail that was posted to De László's address was now being opened and read by the Special Section and reported to MI5. It's clear from later material that a considerable amount of evidence had slipped through the normal censorship system relating to the clandestine sending of messages to his family in Hungary through the Dutch diplomatic bag, and the sending of money to them, also by surreptitious means, must have ended up on MI5's file, but still it did not act. It was most important that its main method of gathering information on suspects remained unknown.

It was only in November 1916 that the normal censorship produced evidence that might be acted upon. An outgoing letter to Madame van Riemsdyk was intercepted in which it was disclosed that De László had apparently sent money to his relatives in Hungary via Madrid. On 5 December 1916, Detective Constable Percy Isaac of Paddington police station was sent to De László's residence to raise the allegation that he had been sending money out of the country. After making several attempts to get his maid to let him in, Isaac announced that he was a detective and was invited in.

De László apologised profusely, saying, 'I am sorry I refused to see you, but I've so many beggars call here that unless a person makes an appointment, I have given instructions that I am not to be seen.' Detective Constable Isaac's report said:

Mr De László stated that his brother Marczel, residing at 28 Eotica Utza, Budapest, has been in need of money. The friend in Madrid, mentioned in the censored letter is Baron Mayendorff member of the Russian Embassy there. The Baron owes Mr P de László £1000 for portrait painting and de László wrote to him asking him to send £200 to his brother Marczel, but he has since heard that his wish has not been complied with.

Mr de László further stated that he had sent money to his brother in Budapest, Hungary, but at the time he was ignorant that he had first to obtain permission.

The last occasion that money was sent from this country was in February last, when Mr de László directed his bankers, London County and Westminster, Lombard Street, City, to forward £500 to Mr Van Riemsdyk, 8 Orange Street, The Hague, Holland, who forwarded the money to Marczel László at Budapest. It was not until he was informed by a friend that he was doing wrong in sending money to an enemy country that he discontinued sending. I would beg to draw notice to the fact that although he knew he had been doing wrong by sending money out of England, he attempts to persuade an ally to send money to his brother.

There was no evidence, after all this time, that De László was a security threat, so on the basis of this report and the other evidence gathered by means of the censorship, the Home Office submitted a case against De László for prosecution under the Trading with the Enemy Act in January 1917. The case was based upon the transmissions of money made to his mother and brothers at various times in 1915 and 1916, and upon the fact that he had been warned against such transactions by Bath Police in February 1915.

As Trading with the Enemy came partially under MI5's remit, on 31 December, MI5's Major Anson sent the Foreign Trade Department a brief summary of the evidence, including D.C. Isaac's report, 'for such action as you think necessary'. The Foreign Trade Department queried Anson's brief letter and asked for further information. Anson sent it copies of the Bath telegram, Inspector Marshfield's report, and a copy of his letter of 25 September 1916. He also suggested an examination of De László's bank account would show further transactions sent to Holland. There was some concern about how De László would react and who his friends were. A note written on the file read, 'Mr De László is pretty certain to write either to Lord Robert [Lord Robert Cecil, Minister of Blockade], or the Secretary for State. As you will notice, he knows Mr Balfour personally and is apparently an MVO.' It was suggested Lord Robert Cecil be consulted and he, in turn, while agreeing that De László should be prosecuted, suggested that it be referred to Mr Balfour, who was now serving as Foreign Secretary. A brief resumé was sent to Mr Balfour, who said that De László had painted him 'twice' and said he was sorry he had got into trouble but added it was not the Foreign Office's business.

The Foreign Trade Department staff certainly felt there was a *prima facie* case to answer. One noted, 'The seriousness of the offence depends upon the total amount sent, but I don't think we can pass over the matter as we have prosecuted for remittance of much smaller sums.' Another added:

It is important to stop such transactions being carried on … It is important that all citizens and naturalized British subjects shall conform to the law … the case would act as a deterrent to others, and illustrate that no object however good, and no motive however well-intentioned can prevail against the law. In this view I think that proceedings should be commenced.

Sir Robert Cecil agreed, but having taken the advice of counsel it was decided an examination of De László's bank account would be required, and a warrant was drawn up authorising an accountant, Mr Wyatt Williams, to examine his records.

Wyatt Williams duly visited De László's residence and examined his books and records. In his report he set out the basic details of the case then gave details of the money transactions overseas. He went on to present his own analysis of what had happened. He explained he thought the Bath Police report was the result of confusion as to the telegram being discussed. The telegram Marshfield had questioned De László about was a follow-up to a previous one attempting to arrange a meeting with his brother, and amended it. Upset at the thought of his mother's death, he had concentrated on the proposed change to the meeting and forgotten about the remittance. It was this confusion and his failure to answer the question properly, said Wyatt Williams, which led Major Anson to think he was lying. As to the other transactions, Wyatt Williams said that in the light of the numerous postcards and letters mentioning the transfers that had passed through censorship, De László had no idea that there was a problem. If there had been, he said, De László thought that the authorities would have advised him. They hadn't, so he assumed he was doing nothing illegal.

Wyatt Williams presented his report on 19 March 1917, and the Department of Foreign Trade officials added their notes. Mr Eady said, 'It is quite clear that an offence has been committed. On the other hand the openness of the correspondence shows that M De László had no idea of his offence, tho' that is no defence.' Mr Spens added, 'I agree, though it is difficult to swallow M. De László's amazing ignorance of very elementary law.' The final comment by Mr Eady is more telling: 'Mr De László is a British subject and must accept the responsibilities of the position. He must inform himself of the law. He has no right to commit a breach of it, as if he were a foreigner whose interests and sympathies lay only abroad.' Turning to the correspondence (all of which MI5 would have had copies of thanks to the Special Measures Censorship, though Eady would not have been aware of this), he went on:

When put together the letters show clearly what was going on; but individually to the censor, many of the letters reveal nothing necessarily amiss and may have been allowed to pass on that ground. Most of the letters do not necessarily indicate an enemy destination for the money and that dated 18th March is the only one, I think, that indicates that the money had come from the UK. Indeed many of the letters are cryptic in their silence as to the origin and destination of the money. After the warnings given in Febry 1915 the plan for remittance by a Russian friend needs further elucidation. I think that all these matters had better be investigated in their proper place when Mr De László will be given a full opportunity of explanation. If he had been born in England he would have been clearly in the wrong.

It was only in June 1917 that the Attorney General decided that no prosecution was to take place, on condition that De László was interviewed by Mr Matthews of the Attorney General's Office, and the gravity of his offence explained to him. The interview duly took place on 18 June, and 'Mr De László very willingly and with expressions of gratitude' signed a solemn undertaking 'never hereafter to send any monetary remittance to my relatives in Hungary, or to any enemy of this country, without first having obtained the sanction of the proper authority'. Whether MI5 continued the special censorship of his mail is uncertain. But events were soon to take a further, and more sinister, series of turns.

3

ALARM
BELLS

O N 7 JULY 1917, MI5 received, via the Bureau Central
Interalliée (Inter-Allied Intelligence Bureau) in Paris,
forwarded by Charles Bigham, British representative
there, a message he'd received from the French secret service.
It read:

> The Austrian services in Switzerland are getting very good
> political information from England by means of Madame
> G. (they have not got her name) who perhaps belongs to the
> Swiss Legation, but certainly possesses a diplomatic passport.
> She sends her correspondence by the Dutch diplomatic bag. It is
> believed that she is already suspected in diplomatic circles in
> London. They would be very glad to hear of any information
> you may have about this.

The Bureau Central Interalliée had been formed in the autumn
of 1915 and was based in the French Ministry of War. There
were, at first, representatives from the intelligence services of
Britain, France, Russia and Belgium, with Italy, Portugal and

the USA joining as they entered the war. Each country was represented by its own intelligence mission. British officers served under SIS though some had previous MI5 experience, as did some of the female clerical staff. The main office was in the Boulevard St Germain, though the British seem to have had a sub office at 30 Avenue Marceau. It was a vast clearing house for information, much of it relating to attempts by the Germans to break the economic blockade, but there was a steady exchange of information on possible enemy agents and their methods.

Charles Clive Bigham, head of the British mission, was another officer with long experience. Born in 1872, eldest son of the first Viscount Mersey, a distinguished high court judge, he was Eton-educated and, against his father's wishes, decided on a career in the army. He spent three years in the Grenadier Guards but found soldiering at home monotonous so transferred to the reserve and toured the Middle East, reporting to the Foreign Office on Turkey, Persia, Russia, China and the Balkans. He spoke six European languages plus some Persian, Turkish and Chinese. He was *Times* correspondent during the 1897 Graeco-Turkish War and an honorary attaché in Constantinople. He was in Manchuria reporting on the new Russian railway when the Boxer Rebellion broke out and he served (with the Foreign Office's permission) with the Russian army. On returning from China, he spent two years in the War Office Intelligence Department, then in the Board of Trade, and stood as Liberal candidate in the 1906 general election, losing Windsor by 200 votes. In 1908 he became secretary of the Free Trade Union and the Home Counties Liberal Federation. On the outbreak of war he was appointed as a staff officer, serving as provost marshal at Gallipoli and then military attaché in Cairo. In 1916 he was appointed head of the intelligence mission in Paris, where his languages, diplomatic work and wide experience stood him in good stead.

Passed to MI5g, the investigation branch, the few details available in Bigham's letter would have been checked against MI5's extensive card index. Checks would have been run, and files pulled, on anyone connected with the Swiss Legation or suspected Dutch subjects in London, particularly women with the initial 'G' and with diplomatic passports. MI5 was certainly aware of alleged attempts to abuse the Dutch diplomatic bag elsewhere – the Singapore censor had identified, from a normal letter sent through the mail, that an Austrian package had been sent via the bag from The Hague to Batavia in the Dutch East Indies in January 1916, and a German writer had referred to receiving mail from the USA in the Dutch bag addressed to Mr Mosselmans in the Dutch Foreign Office in July that year. They were also aware, from some correspondence that had passed the censor in June 1915, that Madame van Riemsdyk, sister of the Dutch foreign minister, and friend of De László, had used the Dutch diplomatic bag to send items to him. An urgent request for any further information would have been sent to the French via Bigham at the Bureau Central Interalliée.

In response, Bigham forwarded a further message from the French secret service, dated 12 July 1917, giving clearer details:

We are informed, from a reliable source, that the Austrian Secret Service in Switzerland gets news through a Dutch subject.

The latter apparently gets his information from one Ph. A. László in London, 3 Palace Gate. László is a painter, Hungarian by birth, British by Naturalization, who has access, apparently, to official circles in England.

The General Staff of the Army has the honour to beg the British Mission to be so good as to keep a close and discreet watch upon László's activities and correspondence.

The General Staff would be grateful, particularly, if he might be shadowed, so that persons whom he meets, and his means of livelihood may be ascertained, and if enquiries may be made as to any journies [sic] to foreign parts, which he may have made since the beginning of the War.

Any journey which he may have made to France should be notified to the French Secret Service (à la S.C.R.) and any useful information relating to him should be collected and sent through to them.

Here, at last was a name, and to MI5 at least, confirmation they'd been right in keeping De László on watch since 1915. The case had moved up several gears, and it's likely that, if he wasn't watched before by MI5's shadowing staff, a watch was put on De László now.

Things had changed since 1914. Melville, the retired Special Branch officer who'd originally run the Detective Branch (as it was known) had taken on a purely advisory role (he was 67 years old), and his original staff had been gradually augmented until it stood at ten by the end of 1916. In 1917, Colonel Ormerod took over the section and suitable men were drafted in from MI5's Ports Police until the number stood at about 30. The section was split and renamed P1 and P2, and, as a subsequent report says, 'the average time of 14 days which had elapsed before reports of enquiries were received from Special Branch was reduced … to one or two days for ordinary enquiries'.

The staff, some of whom excelled at observation work, comprised men from a wide range of backgrounds. There were solicitors, a bank employee, hotel manager, journalist, commercial travellers and a music publisher. Among them was Harry Hunter, who continued to work for MI5 between the wars and who ran B6 section (as it was then known) throughout the Second World War. MI5 probably now had details of every visitor to De László's studio, of his own movements during the day, as well as full-time access to everything delivered by the Royal

Mail. It would be interesting to know whether they observed the next development. Unfortunately the Home Office files don't say either way.

On Monday 16 July 1917, a brief notice appeared in *The Times*, which read, 'Three prisoners of war escaped from Donington Hall on Saturday evening.' Two were German naval officers, Karl Spindler and Max Ernest Winkelman. The third was an Austrian military officer, Arped Horn, described as 'aged 28, complexion fair, dark hair, eyes dark brown, stout build, height 5ft 6 ½ inches, short stubby moustache, dress probably civilian, mole on face'. Another officer was caught on the barbed wire by guards. The two Germans were captured the same day by a policeman in Nottingham who caught them using a public drinking fountain, but Horn remained free.

On Wednesday 18 July at about 1.40 p.m., a foreign-sounding gentleman presented himself at the desk of Kensington police station and was initially interviewed by Constable Alexander Allan. He told him that at 12.30 p.m. on 17 July, Arped Horn, the escaped Austrian officer from Donington Hall, called at his studio, West House, 118 Camden Hill Road, Kensington.

According to Allan's written statement, dated the next day and witnessed by Acting Superintendent W. MacMillan:

Mr László De Lombas informed me that when Horn called, he handed in a letter asking to see him. The letter was written in Hungarian. Mr László De Lombas saw him and Horn told him who he was, and that he was staying at the Golden Cross as an American. Horn asked for money and Mr László De Lombas gave him £1, and stated that he was so upset at seeing Horn that it did not occur to him to inform Police until after Horn had left. He then stated that he forgot the name of the hotel where Horn said he was staying, until the following morning when he found the envelope of the letter in the waste paper basket: the envelope bore the name of the Golden Cross Hotel. Mr László De Lombas stated that he did not know Horn prior to his call, he gave his description and promised to communicate with Police should he ever hear anything of him again.

Acting on the instructions of Sergeant Sudbury (CID), PC Allan and Sergeant Warner (CID) were sent to meet Sergeant Fred Warner (CID) from Bow Street station at the hotel on the Strand.

PC Allen met Sergeant Fred Warner from Bow Street outside the Golden Cross Hotel at 2.30 p.m., explained why he thought Horn was in the hotel and gave him a description. The manager, Mr Blissett, produced the hotel register and, upon examination, Warner noticed one guest had spelled his name Georg Chapman and that 'the writing on the registration form ... appeared to be foreign'. The hotel book-keeper was asked for a description of Chapman and it matched that of Horn. Chapman was out, so Warner went to his room and, on examining his luggage, found an Austrian or Hungarian tunic in a small attaché case. Warner and Allen waited for his return. In the meantime, Sergeant Fred Warner went to West House at 118 Camden Hill Road, and kept observation to see if Horn called on De László again.

The suspect returned to the hotel at about 5.45 p.m., and Sergeant Warner said to him, 'Your name is Chapman and you are an American', to which he replied, 'Yes.' When asked for his papers, however, he replied, 'I have none.' Warner then said, 'Then you must be Arped Horn' and Chapman admitted the fact. The two policemen identified themselves and arrested him. He was taken to Blissett's office, searched and allowed to pay his bill, which he did with English money, leaving him with about three pounds. He was taken to Bow Street police station, where he was detained until a military escort arrived and took him back to Donington Hall. No action seems to have been taken against De László at this point.

Further information on the arrangements used by the alleged spies was received on 24 July:

> The news sent from Madam G. goes apparently to an individual known as 'l'ami hollondais' and from him to the Austro-Hungarian Military Attaché at Berne. By the same means László the painter, who is principally concerned with pacifist propaganda, is also supposed to be in communication with the latter. It is thought that Madam G. is suspicious of being watched as on June 20th it is remarked that 'another method of correspondence must be found'.

The Berne connection would hardly have surprised MI5; the previous year, they'd helped break up a joint German-Japanese espionage ring based there that was obtaining information on the Royal Navy from Japanese officers in their London Embassy who were, apparently, bribing a naval officer. Though Japan and Germany were at war, British agents in Switzerland were able to show a close connection between other Japanese officers and the German and Austrian legations. Japan might also have had an interest in sharing information on the Royal Navy, even with an enemy, with a view to expanding her own navy.

Switzerland, as a neutral country bordering Germany and Austria of the Central Powers, and France and Italy of the Allied nations, was central to both sides' espionage activities, much of which was based in their consulates. The British used consulate-based military control officers, who issued visas to Swiss and other foreigners hoping to travel to Britain, as the basis of their more formal secret service organisation, but also employed many secret agents among businessmen, journalists and regular visitors to the country. The German and Austrian organisation was similar but seems to have relied rather more on the consulates. Penetration of, or even physical assault upon, these consulates was vital in the secret war being carried out under the noses of the ever-vigilant Swiss police. In March 1917, the Italian secret service scored a spectacular coup when it burgled the Commercial and Military Department of the Austrian Consulate in Zurich. A group broke into the department, which occupied the whole second floor of a large building in the Bahnhofstrasse, and stole 50,000 Austrian Crowns in banknotes and a further 20,000 Crowns in gold. They also stripped the department of every piece of paper in the place, estimated to weigh over a ton. To do so, they had managed to penetrate steel and concrete, combination locks and secret defences including asphyxiating gas by using liquid air, hydrogen, oxygen, electric drills, gas masks and special screens to mask the sound. The whole operation took over a day. Papers stolen in the robbery were used in a number of trials of enemy agents in Italy over the course of the next year, their source being disguised by the claim the papers had been purchased from the criminals.

The Austrian military attaché in Berne was Colonel William von Einem, who was certainly involved in espionage and propaganda duties. He worked closely with Captain Rudolph Meyer of the Imperial-Royal Navy, regularly received information on the Italian army from Colonel Elgi, head of Swiss military intelligence, and ran agents and propaganda material into Italy. Von Einem's agents provided accurate details of Italian offensives, sabotaged a munitions factory and sank two warships. One of his better agents was Angelica Balabanoff, a Russian socialist exile with influence over the pro-peace Italian Socialist Party. Von Einem was a natural target for the allies' intelligence services, and, if the French really did have an agent with access to his papers, this would have been a real coup. Though happy to share information, there was a mutual agreement that, for security reasons, secret agents' identities should remain secret, even from friends.

At this point, events take a slightly strange turn. An 'agent of Mr Basil Thomson' produced a copy of a letter from Geneva dated 14 June 1917 which he (or she) had been able to obtain. Addressed to 'Monsieur Ph. A. LÁSZLÓ, Palace Gate, 3, Londres', it read:

Dear Friend,

Your kind letter of May 30 reached me, as well as your most interesting information. Many thanks for your friendly attentions. Where are the days when we were both bursting with youth? But now for serious matters.

I forwarded to the Legation to be allowed to resume your Hungarian Nationality. I have no doubt but that it will be granted; you have rendered such important services to the Monarchy that you have earned a favour of this kind.

With this letter you will receive documents relating to the treatment of German prisoners in France. Do what is necessary to make the revolting facts known in Society, at Court, and in intellectual circles.

Your report of yesterday confirms what I have said of you for a long time. You have in you the stuff of which diplomats, clever business men, and journalists are made. The report is of the highest importance, and gives a splendid picture of the true picture in England.

I have only one thing to ask you, Don't mention Madame G in your letters any more.

There is a highly placed personage who cannot forgive her for being the wife of an Ambassador, seeing she was only a Jewess. Call on her frequently; what you get from her is also worth having.

With the letter came an attachment, which, if the statement in it was true, really could have caused problems:

I have just received, through our 'Dutch friend', the attached Report drawn out by L (A.O.) The report is extremely valuable; in particular it gives the exact dates of the losses of ships belonging to Great Britain, figures and statistics relative to the critical condition of the mining industry, and a true idea of the views held at court. *If it is true – and the authenticity of L's information cannot be doubted – that the King is visibly, and increasingly desirous of seeing the War at an end, and that he has said, apparently, that Alsace Lorraine was not worth an hour's prolongation of the War, peace cannot be far off now.*

L attached to his report a few lines for me. He begs me to ask the Authorities whether he cannot recover his Hungarian Nationality after the War. Please answer me as to this, and I will send it on to him.

I am contenting myself to-day with telling him that I will look after him, and with expressing my personal opinion that his request cannot but meet with a favourable reception, in view of the great services which he rendered us last year.

May I add, to give you the true perspective, that L has already sent in nearly 40 reports, which money will not pay for. L's success has been rapid; as a converted Jew he had the entrée to Pope Leo the 13th's presence, and shortly afterwards to the German Court, and the British Court. Hence he has a number of enemies, who made his life impossible in Hungary.

It is not identified who Thomson's agent was, but there is one fascinating possibility. On the outbreak of war, Thomson had taken on a private enquiry agency run by the

---

* Such was the controversy likely to have been caused if this section of the report came out that it was deleted in the copies later supplied to Messrs Chas. Russell & Co. (De László's solicitors) and in the copies for the use of the Denaturalisation Committee.

theatrical impresario Maundy Gregory to do the most basic work of enquiring about visitors to hotels and running errands. Gregory later became famous as the only man ever to be found guilty of selling honours on behalf of the government to raise money for political purposes. On 13 June 1917, being just within the age range for conscription, Gregory was conscripted and a couple of days later actually enlisted at Windsor. A few weeks later, he tried for a commission in the Intelligence or Secret Services, but was rebuffed by both MI5 and SIS. He claimed, however, as part of his attempt, that not only had he run his enquiry agency on behalf of the authorities, but had received a government grant to do so. The dates don't quite fit, but it is possible that passing on a copy of this letter might have been his final service in this capacity. Whoever it was that copied it or when, there is a note in the file discussing whether De László had received it, reading, 'there is no doubt at all that he did.'

At some point, a further piece of correspondence copied from the German Legation appeared to be a letter addressed to it from Geneva. It was dated 16 July 1917. Clearly marked as 'Secret', it read:

I respectfully request you to pass on the following to Frau Gomperz for Ph. A. László, London, Palace Gte, 3:-
'Your report that you have the feeling of being watched makes me beg you before all not to undertake anything more, and to keep perfectly quiet.

After some time of rest and quiet I shall advise you further.'

With best thanks

One has to wonder whether De László had spotted MI5's shadowing staff keeping an eye on him.

It was only on 24 July that a letter from Madame van Riemsdyk, stating that she was forwarding something 'by the ordinary route', was intercepted, probably by the ordinary censorship, as at some point in July they placed all her mail under check for the first time. It was clear from this letter that De László had been communicating with Madame van Riemsdyk by some channel other than the ordinary post – presumably the Dutch diplomatic bag. Now MI5 had evidence it could use in open court of the link between De László and use of the bag, and, if nothing else, a serious breach of the censorship regulations. This would allow them to keep their own monitoring of his mail secret and allow them to prosecute if necessary.

4

THE FIRST
INTERROGATION

THE CASE AGAINST De László was now building up, and on
15 August 1917, he was examined at New Scotland Yard
by Basil Thomson, Mr Curtis Bennett and Major Carter
of MI5, Lord Herschell, government chief whip in the House of
Lords, and Mr Ralph Hughes-Buller, a former director of criminal intelligence in India who was attached to Scotland Yard on
'special duties'.

The MI5 officers who took part (though they seem to have
sat silent throughout) were both highly experienced in counter-
espionage work. Major John Fillis Carre Carter, born 1882, had
joined MI5 on the day war broke out after fourteen years' service
in the Indian army and Burmese police. He had seen active service in Waziristan in 1901–02 and had been with the Burmese
police since 1905. Like all Indian army officers, he spoke two
Indian languages (Punjabi and Pushtu) as well as Burmese
and Kachin. He had served in MI5's Investigation Branch
since the day he joined and had become head of G Branch in
February 1917 when his predecessor, Reggie Drake, transferred
to France to run the army's Secret Intelligence Service I(b).

Accompanying him was Lieutenant Henry Honywood Curtis-Bennett, Royal Naval Volunteer Reserve, a 38-year-old barrister who had been educated at Radley College and Trinity College, Cambridge, before being called to the Bar in 1902. He had joined MI5 in January 1917 after being recommended for the work by Sir Archibald Bodkin, Director of Public Prosecutions, who was a personal friend. He joined the RNVR and was almost immediately appointed to the Naval Intelligence Division 'for duty outside the Admiralty', a standard euphemism for officers attached to either MI5 or the Secret Intelligence Service.

The usual caution was administered to De László, and Basil Thomson led off the questioning. According to the transcript he did all the speaking on behalf of the authorities. Where direct quotes are given at length, he is ACC (Assistant Commissioner Crime) and De László is PAL:

ACC   Did not a prisoner of war come to your house some
        time ago?
PAL   Yes, to my studio, HORN, who escaped from the camp.
ACC   Did you at once give information to the police?
PAL   No.
ACC   Why?
PAL   It was such a surprise to me for a man I had never seen
        before to come to me like that. I was painting and my
        servant girl brought up a letter. I do not usually see
        people when I am painting, but I went down. The man
        said 'I am a Hungarian officer, and in need of money.'
        I said 'Tell me quickly who you are and what you want,
        for my time is precious.' He said 'I am the man who
        escaped from the concentration camp.' I said 'How
        could you come to me like this?' He said 'Could you not
        give me some money?' I said 'What will you do? Why
        have you escaped?' He said 'I have been so long interned;

I could not stand it any longer.' I said 'No, I cannot give
you money.' But he went on worrying me. I know that
in any case I should have to give him up, but I felt that
I could not do it immediately. I said 'Where do you
live?' and he answered 'In such and such an hotel' (a very
good hotel). I said 'How can you live there if you have
no money?' He said 'I have a certain amount.' So I gave
him £1 just to get rid of him, for I felt that if I did not
give him anything he would feel it. It came to me so
suddenly; it was a psychological moment. He was a
Hungarian, and he looked very nice. I felt I could not go
and telephone to the Police immediately, and give him
up, so that he knew of it, so I said 'Here is £1, now go.'

The letter he had written to me was on hotel paper, but
he took that letter with him. I was so excited about the
whole thing that he had disappeared with the letter before
I realised it. As soon as my sitting was over, about a quarter
to one, I went to the Police, and told them the whole thing.
I asked the man how he knew my address. He found it
in a book; my name is in all the books of reference.

I cannot understand him, because I said to him,
'You are an intelligent man; how can you come to me
like this, knowing I am a British subject, to put me in a
position like this?'

He was in a very excited state, so I gave him the
money and told him to go away.

I am very sorry. I understand now that I did wrong in
giving him money, but I beg you to consider the situation.
Being a Hungarian subject, I had so many unpleasantnesses.
This man came absolutely unexpectedly and I knew I had
to give him up. It is not a pleasant thing to see a fellow in
that situation, being a Hungarian, and speaking Hungarian
(he wrote a very good letter) it would have been very

difficult for me to give nothing at all. (László then spoke of the feeling against himself in Hungary, and continued) Now I thought that if I gave that man up, he would let it be known in Hungary after the war that I had done so, therefore, I did not want him to know it. It was very cruel of the man to put me in that position.

Then I was unhappy all the afternoon. It was a very unpleasant experience for me, as I did not know what to do and had no address.

Before the man left, he said to me 'Is there any other Hungarian whom I could see?'

He pressed me and, knowing I had to give him up, I said 'Yes, there is another Hungarian here, whom you could see, a man called de Boyser, the brother in law of Hughes Hughes, one of the Directors of the Musical Department at the British Museum. His wife and brother are Hungarian.'

Miss Joyce, and the Baroness van Linden, both of Austrian nationality, are great friends of ours, and they gave me the address of de Boyser, writing it down on that very paper. I could not tell them what had happened, as it would have put me in an unpleasant situation. So I gave the man that bit of paper and said 'You can go there.'

These two ladies saw that letter, and I said 'It is an Austrian officer who has come to beg for money.' They looked at the address and said 'It is a good hotel.'

I said to my wife in the evening 'That man came to me, and I have to give him up.'

As soon as I got to the studio the next morning I told the girl to look for the envelope, as I had not been able to find it the previous night, after the sitting of the two ladies was finished at about 5.30.

> The girl went down to the kitchen, and found the
> envelope amongst the rubbish and brought it to me.
> By that I knew the name of the hotel.

Thomson then turned to László's letters to his family, asking whether he had a good many relations in Hungary.

De László replied that yes, he did, and corresponded with two brothers and a sister through Holland. When he was asked about his loyalty, he said:

> I cannot explain what the feeling is, because they behaved so
> very badly at home. Everything is exaggerated. My pictures, one
> of which is known world-wide, have been taken down from the
> Museum. A little while back I had a letter from my brother to
> say that this picture, which I painted for the Government and
> sent to the Pope, has been reinstated, but amongst the pictures
> in the Foreign Section. Now I thought that if I gave that man
> up, he would let it be known in Hungary after the war that I had
> done so, therefore I did not want him to know it. It was very
> cruel of the man to put me in that position.

Asked about friends in Europe he had painted he replied:

> I stayed three times with the German Emperor – I was first invited
> in 1889 – I painted nearly all the Princes. Now I have no corre-
> spondents except my own people. I have great friends in Holland,
> in the Hague Madame van Riemsdyk and others are great friends
> of mine and the letters go through them to Hungary.

Asked whether he wrote to friends in Italy he said he had some but did not write to them, only to friends in the USA and to his family in Hungary. He did not correspond with friends in Spain, visited France for five months every year and had no friends in Switzerland.

In Holland he was great friends with the van Riemsdyks and confirmed that Madame van Riemsdyk was the sister of the Dutch foreign minister, but that he himself wasn't related to her.

Thomson then turned to the use of the diplomatic bag and the questions became tougher:

ACC   I suppose that it is on account of her relationship to the Foreign Minister that you occasionally have had the advantage of sending letters through the Legation Bag?

PAL   Yes. I have not sent many letters that way, but Madame Riemsdyk wrote to me at the beginning of last year that I could get letters that way, because she knows how attached I am to my people. She asked me if I would go to Mr van Swinderen, whom I knew a little, and he promised to send letters for me, but I have not sent letters that way any more than probably five times at the most. In August of last year I went to see Mr van Swinderen and while I was there someone rang him up on the telephone and I heard him say 'O, about those letters – they do not like it at the Foreign Office.' After he had finished speaking on the telephone I said to him 'That means you do not care about forwarding my letters.' He replied 'I will send this letter for you, and any others you forward to me, unless you hear from me to the contrary.' However I never sent him any letters after that.

ACC   I suppose you got letters from Madame van Riemsdyk by the same route?

PAL   Yes, and I wrote to her twice not to send me any more letters through the Dutch Minister because the authorities did not like it. When I was staying in Holland we became great friends. I have painted the du Toits, Lewis van Lowden. I know her brother-in-law. He is a director of the National Museum in Amsterdam.

ACC   But you were writing to her by the ordinary post pretty often?

PAL   Yes. But I have not done it more than four or five times through the Dutch Minister, and I wrote a letter to her every month.

ACC   But since you were writing to her almost voluminously by the ordinary route, why should it be necessary to send other letters through the Minister's Bag?

PAL   In the beginning of the war I asked her if she could help me to get letters. Then she offered to send letters this way, because they arrive sooner. She simply said, 'I have the opportunity through my brother, to send you letters quicker, through the bag.'

ACC   You were writing practically once a fortnight?

PAL   It happened now and then that I was lucky and received three letters in succession, which were forwarded to me: one from my sister one from a great nephew of mine and one from my brother, so I answered within a week.

Thomson then asked a question that must have given the game away that the correspondence was being monitored, asking 'Who was Madame G in those letters?', to which De László (as MI5 noticed) replied, 'I do not remember who it can have been. It may have been someone in the Corps Diplomatique.' He did not deny her existence. He gave a couple of Dutch names (neither of which began with G), and Thomson expanded, 'I think the lady in question was supposed to be of Jewish extraction originally.' De László replied, 'It is so against my custom to use an initial in a letter – I do not know what it can be. It must have been a long time ago.' Thomson admitted it was. Madame de Youngichaen, a Hungarian lady related to the Rothschilds and living in Switzerland, was briefly discussed and discounted before Thomson turned to the criminal regulations regarding corresponding without going through the censored channels:

ACC   Of course, Mr László, you have been perfectly open about
        having sent letters that way, but I ought to read you this
        Regulation [Thomson then read out DORA Regulation
        R24 with regard to transmitting letters without lawful
        authority by means other than through the post].

PAL   I have no answer to give. It is unfortunate, but I did
        not know it was against a regulation. My conscience
        is absolutely clear I never said anything in a letter that
        I ought not to have said.

ACC   That is not the point. The thing is you ought not to
        have sent the letters that way.

PAL   My position is such as an artist and the father of five
        boys that I give you my word of honour that I never in
        my life have written a word that was against my feeling
        as a man, or that I ought not to have done.

The position having been made clear, Thomson turned again to
his loyalty and whether he desired peace:

PAL   Certainly I do, for Hungary always was friendly to
        England. If you ask me as to political matters, it is a
        very sad situation for the Hungarians – they have to
        fight. They were very ambitious to fight when Roumania
        attacked them, but Hungary up to now was always
        devoted to England. I talked with a Prime Minister in
        Hungary whom I painted some time ago about these
        things, because I visited a young Hungarian who is
        interned here. This man came over to give a concert with
        his wife and children at the Queen's Hall, and he was
        here when the *Lusitania* went down and they interned
        him. I said to him, 'Page, you ought not to be interned,
        because no British subject is interned in Hungary.
        All British subjects are regarded as honorary guests

there.' So far as my knowledge goes, there is no British subject interned in Hungary. The feeling between the two nations was very intimate. We lived there only a year after we were married. The Hungarians are a sporting people like the British and live in the same way.

There was a brief discussion over the treatment of prisoners of war and Thomson turned back to correspondents abroad:

ACC You said just now that you had no communication with anybody in Switzerland or Spain. Is that quite correct?

PAL I have no communication at all. I received one letter from my brother-in-law via Switzerland at the beginning of the war. I remember now the name of that lady whose daughter was married to an Englishman; it was Mr Michaels. They wanted a separation, and she wrote a letter to me from Switzerland on this matter to explain to me her situation. Then she sent another letter to my wife – a very long letter, like a book (I cannot understand how the censor had the patience to go through it). We destroyed it immediately because we did not want to have anything to do with them. Mrs Michaels sent a letter twice, but received no answer from us. I received one letter from my brother-in-law and these two from Madame Michaels.

ACC But was there not a proposal at one time that you should send money to your brother through some friend in Spain?

PAL Yes, Baron Mayendorff.

ACC That led to some correspondence?

PAL Yes.

ACC That is a correction of your original statement?

PAL No, nothing came via Switzerland. Baron Mayendorff was here at the Russian Embassy and I made his acquaintance through Miss Warrender, whose life sized portrait I painted. Then I did some painting in Paris in January 1914, and then we went to Italy and I was invited by the King of Greece to paint the whole family. The Baroness wanted me to paint her husband's portrait; I commenced this but was not able to complete it, so, as I told them I always come to London twice a year, it was arranged that I would finish it in my London studio. Then of course the war broke out and I heard nothing of them until August or September of last year when I had a message from the Ritz Hotel where they were living. 'Would I finish the portrait now?' I agreed, so he came, and his uniform is still at my studio. I asked them to lunch with me, as they had been here for a long time, seven years, and I had lunched with them a few times. They were going back to Zurich where they always lived in the summer. His wife has property there, and his brother is, I think, in the Russian Embassy there ... He asked me if he could do anything for me. I said 'Yes, I cannot send money to my brother. If you could send it over for me, I should be very pleased if you would.' He said 'Certainly, with the greatest pleasure.' I gave him a letter. He took the letter and the cheque, and promised that the money should remain here. He said 'They talk so much about you, so, if you can; if not, send it back.' I gave him my cheque on the London County and Westminster Bank.

ACC   To the police officer who visited you, you said 'The Baron owes Mr P de László £1,000 for portrait painting , and Mr de László wrote asking him to send £200 to his brother, Marczel, but he has since heard that this wish has not been complied with.' Is that right?

PAL   No, when he was in my studio I could not finish the picture so I did not ask for money. He owed me £1,000.

ACC   But in this case you said you had written to him asking
      him to send £200 to your brother.

PAL   That is wrong. I could not have said that. I never
      wrote to him … I said 'I give you a cheque for £200,
      but the money must remain in England.' I asked him
      how he would send it to my brother, and he said 'If I
      cannot send it though the Minister my wife is going
      to Switzerland to see my brother. She will stay there
      several weeks and she will arrange it, or I am expecting
      my brother here and I will ask him to forward it.'
      At any rate, I had a letter from my brother about a
      month ago, in which he said he had not received
      any money.

ACC   Why did you say anything to the police officer about
      Mayendorff owing you money unless it was to imply
      that he was to pay what he owed you? As a matter of fact,
      was the cheque ever cashed?

PAL   That I do not know. I have not looked out my pass book.

ACC   You have not satisfied yourself as to whether the money
      was drawn?

PAL   I think it was, because Mr Williams {the accountant
      appointed by the Home Office earlier in the year}
      looked through my books.

Thomson then produced a copy of a letter that does not appear
to be extant on the surviving file:

ACC   Did you ever see that letter? (Exhibit A – Photograph of
letter to Mayendorff.)

PAL   I really do not remember that letter.

ACC   I suggest to you that it was delivered or posted by someone in London. It came through a man named Taylor.

PAL   I have never heard that name.

A further question about De László's exact relationship with Madame van Riemsdyk established that her daughter Daisy called him Uncle Philip, but that she was no relation really.

Thomson then turned back to more intercepted correspondence, asking, 'Do you know a young woman called Miss Lundquist?' It was established she was Anna Lundquist, Swedish and his house-keeper, having previously been his wife's maid. She had left because of problems with the other servants, but had recently returned to look after the house while the family were in Datchet. De László did not know where she had been in the interim. It was also estab-lished that she, too, was corresponding with someone in Holland, though De László denied any knowledge of this:

ACC   Well, I will tell you what happened. A postcard was
      received for her addressed to your house on the 14th
      July (that would be all right if she went to you on the
      6th) except that it is a little difficult to know how her
      correspondent in Holland should have known. After
      this postcard was received, the police asked her to
      call, and she then gave her address as 14 Holland Park,
      and said nothing about ever being employed by you.
PAL   That is very strange. I know she has a friend in the Army
      who she knew years before the war broke out who sends
      her postcards and letters. He is an Englishman.
ACC   (Postcard in question read to him.) Who is L?
PAL   I do not know.
ACC   The writer of this is known to us and very unfavourably
      known, and he addresses it to your house. How could
      he have known that she was at your house if she had not
      been there for years before now?

Quite who the mysterious writer was, or why he was unfavourably known to MI5, is not stated on the files. Thomson then turned

again to De László's attitude to Hungary, and in the course of the
interrogation things turned very serious. It is given here verbatim:

ACC I understand you have a hereditary title granted by the
      Emperor of Austria?

PAL   By the King of Hungary really.

ACC Yes, and I suppose that on naturalisation as a British
      subject you parted with that title did you not?

PAL   I do not think so. I applied first of all for naturalisation
      before the war. Mr Balfour, Lord Devonport, my brother-
      in-law Howard Guinness are my sponsors. I intended to
      become naturalised two years before the war broke out,
      and many people knew of it. Then it happened that I went
      to Balfour just before the war broke out, and we talked
      about things. I said that I had very great esteem for the old
      Emperor Joseph who was very nice, and that I preferred
      postponing my naturalisation until after his death. When
      the war broke out a Hungarian who I had never seen
      before came over to England because he thought it was
      the safest place for a Hungarian to be. He brought me a
      letter of recommendation from an old friend of mine. I was
      so pleased to learn from this letter that my mother was
      still alive that I gave him a letter to take back, which was,
      however taken away from him. He was the very man whom
      I invited to lunch with me. He went home and made a
      big story out of it. He asked me what my position was and
      I said 'I am a British subject.' (This was not then known in
      Hungary, it came out afterwards.) Then this man went back
      to Hungary and made a terrible row in the papers, and only
      one man stood for me, a very reliable good friend of mine
      from whom I have had four or five letters during the war –
      Baron Forster – who looks after art matters in Hungary.
      He wrote that there was a meeting at the Art Academy

called together on my account. He said 'They were all
down on you and I stood beside you, and brought it so far
that they said they would not go against you altogether.'

ACC Otherwise they look on you as a traitor?

PAL Yes.

ACC How did those letters from Baron Forster come?

PAL Probably one or two through the ordinary post.
They were always written in French.

ACC Where were they written?

PAL Once he sent me a postcard with a picture of his estate in
Hungary and that was written in Vienna. He was here a
year before the war broke out.

ACC I suppose the letters came through Switzerland?

PAL I do not know.

ACC How did they actually reach you?

PAL From the Dutch Minister. I think the very first letter
which reached me came through his wife. He has a
son who was in Switzerland with his wife and he said
'My wife will forward you this letter.' That was the only
letter I received from him via Switzerland.

ACC I suppose it was rather painful for you to be accused of
being a traitor to Hungary where you had an established
reputation. It would be very convenient for you to have
a dual nationality.

PAL I never thought of that. I am a British subject and my
five sons are British.

ACC I am going to suggest to you that you have in your mind
the idea of resumption of Hungarian nationality after
the war.

PAL I do not believe I have.

ACC I think you have expressed that wish in a letter.

PAL I do not remember ever having expressed a wish like that.

ACC It would be a solution to all your difficulties in Hungary.

PAL   I never thought of that.

ACC   You wrote a letter on the 30th of May to a friend in Switzerland and in that letter you said that you would like to recover your Hungarian nationality. Of course you may have said that with the object of tempering down this storm against you in Hungary.

PAL   To whom could I have written that, because I have no friends in Switzerland? Could I have answered the letter to Baron Forster in Switzerland?

ACC   You do not keep copies of your letters, do you?

PAL   No.

ACC   Did you hear from Baron Forster in May of this year?

PAL   Probably. I think I had a letter from him this year.

ACC   Do you keep your letters?

PAL   I keep all my letters. Mr Williams was asked to look after my papers. He is a chartered accountant.

ACC   What is his address?

PAL   Somewhere in the city – I do not know where.

ACC   Where would you put all your letters?

PAL   They are in my house at 3 Palace Gate. I left a key there.

ACC   I suggest that it was in a letter to Baron Forster that you intimated that you would like to recover your Hungarian nationality.

PAL   I do not believe that I have written such words: my feelings are such that it would be impossible for me to do so. If I was a single man it might have been easier, but I could not play such a game on my children.

ACC   It is not suggested that you would alter your sons' nationality or even your own.

PAL   They accuse me of being a traitor to my country – I have all these letters – Baron Forster is on my side.

ACC   As a matter of diplomacy with the Hungarians you might have intimated that in your letter.

PAL   I do not think so. I do not know what they feel about me in Hungary. In my brother-in-law's last letter received about three weeks ago, he says that a man whom I knew many years ago – a restorer of old modern pictures – came to him and said 'I knew your brother Philip, but I have had nothing to do with him for a number of years. They have decided to put his pictures among the foreign artists.'

ACC   Did your letters from Baron Forster come through Madame van Riemsdyk?

PAL   Yes.

ACC   And probably through the Legation Bag?

PAL   One or two probably.

ACC   I suppose you answered them by the same medium?

PAL   Yes.

ACC   How many letters do you think you have written to Baron Forster all together?

PAL   Five, six or possibly seven. I am not sure.

ACC   You said just now that you sent through the Legation Bag altogether about six, so I take it those are the six. As a matter of fact none of the Forster letters came by post.

PAL   I gave him the address to send them to Madame van Riemsdyk.

ACC   They came through the Legation Bag?

PAL   I cannot say if they all did.

ACC   I suggest to you that they all went through the Legation Bag.

PAL   It is probable. I will not say yes or no.

ACC   I suggest to you that that was the reason you used the Legation Bag in order to send letters to Baron Forster in Vienna.

PAL   Yes, I was invited by Madame van Riemsdyk to do it.

ACC   But why did you not say so the first time we got on to the subject this morning? You said they were all ordinary letters, and suggested they were letters to your family.

PAL   I have been so much irritated already. I showed them all
the letters. I take it for granted you know all about me.

ACC   It is a very serious matter. Here you are communicating
with an enemy through a Legation Bag.

PAL   My conscience is absolutely clear.

ACC   Your conscience may be clear, but my mind is not clear
at all about this.

PAL   I am very sorry about it. I did it in good faith.

Thomson then raised the subject of sending information to the
enemy and began to worm out to whom it was sent and who
Madame G was:

ACC   I will put this to you – you wrote on the 30th of May
sending certain information and saying that you would
like to recover your Hungarian nationality.

PAL   I send information? What information?

ACC   I am putting the question to you – political information
on the state of the country.

PAL   Never in my life have I mentioned even to my brother
about the war.

ACC   Did Baron Forster in any of his letters say anything to
you about the treatment of prisoners of war in France?

PAL   I do not remember Baron Forster or anyone else
doing so. No, I know nothing about it. I have never
corresponded about the war at all.

ACC   Did he write to you on the ardent desire in Hungary
for peace?

PAL   I do not remember – I possess all his letters.

ACC   He was going to put forward for you the claim that you
had rendered services to the Hungarian government –
of course that might be in the way of paintings and
so forth.

PAL   It is very difficult for me to talk of my own merits,
       but I have all honours which an artist can possess in
       Hungary, in Austria and, I may say, in Europe, and I
       received the French Legion of Honour, about thirteen
       years ago. I received all the high prizes before I was
       introduced for this Legion of Honour.

ACC   When you wrote to Baron Forster what did you put on
       the letters?

PAL   'To His Excellency Baron Jules Forster'. Probably
       one time I would put 'Member of the House of
       Lords' etc etc.

ACC   What address?

PAL   I write to his address in Budapest.

ACC   Was there no intermediary address in Switzerland?

PAL   No.

ACC   I suggest to you that you have received a letter addressed
       from Geneva.

PAL   That was probably from Madame Michaels who lives there
       with her daughter. As I mentioned before, I received one
       letter from Baron Forster through his wife who was staying
       in Switzerland with her son. No other letters came from
       Switzerland, except one of my brother-in-law's to a firm,
       which I never used. Then I received through Switzerland
       those two letters, as I told you, from Madame Michaels.

ACC   Did Madame Michaels mention anything about the
       recovery of your Hungarian nationality?

PAL   No, we [are] not on sufficiently familiar terms for that.

ACC   I suggest to you that you did receive a letter from
       Geneva dealing with the question of your nationality.
       Who was it from?

PAL   I do not remember. I received no other letters than
       the ones I have mentioned. I sent a letter to my sister
       Rosa two or three days ago which I put in an envelope.

Sometimes I leave her letters without an envelope, because my brother gives it to my sister. She sent me her address in Budapest, so I put it in an envelope addressed to her.

ACC I am speaking now of the letters to Baron Forster.

PAL They were sent in an envelope addressed to him to Madame Riemsdyk and she would forward them by post. She told me she sent them on by post. Once or twice she was kind enough to send a telegram – when my mother died for instance. We sent her £2 or £3 for the expenses and she sends the letters registered.

ACC I put it to you that in one of your letters you wrote to somebody abroad, you sent a true picture of the situation in England – the political situation.

PAL Never in my life.

ACC Therefore if anybody wrote to you thanking you for this report they would be trying to lead you into a trap?

PAL Nobody wrote to me about it: nobody asked me about political matters.

ACC Has anybody written to you in Hungarian from Switzerland?

PAL I do not remember if that letter from my brother-in-law was written in Hungarian: he sent the first letter via Switzerland.

ACC Who was the Duchess de Guise?

PAL She died about 13 or 14 years ago and the Duke is married to a second wife who is Italian.

ACC Do you visit the Duchess de Guise when you are in Paris?

PAL I live there; we are the most intimate friends.

ACC Could anybody in correspondence with you have referred to her as 'Madame G'? Could you in any of your letters to people abroad have mentioned the Duchess de Guise?

PAL   Now I remember. You asked me if I had a friend in
Italy. I had two letters during the war from Madame
de Martino, whose portrait I painted before the war.

ACC   I do not think that is the thing. I was wondering whether
in your correspondence you ever mentioned the Duchess
de Guise as Madame de Guise in the French fashion.

PAL   No. There are no other people with whom I have been
in correspondence.

ACC   Is Madame de Guise pessimistic about the war?

PAL   I do not know. My friend never wrote about the war: nor
did I have any correspondence with his wife.

ACC   Do you happen to know Madame Carlin, the wife of the
Swiss Minister here?

PAL   No, but I met him once.

ACC   You knew he was married?

PAL   I met him once, that is all: I never met her.

ACC   Do you know anybody named Madame Gompertz,
the daughter of an Austrian banker?

PAL   No.

(Some letters and a diary were handed over for investigation and
Mr László was asked to leave the room for a few minutes)

On his return, Thomson showed De László great consideration
by allowing him to go back to his studio and work:

We cannot consider this matter as cleared up in any way, but I do
not want to upset your arrangements this afternoon, so I want
to put this to you, that you should go and lunch now where you
like, but that you should go with Inspector Parker: for I must
be in a position to say that you have not been out of sight of
an officer. Further, that Inspector Parker should be about your
studio this afternoon and you must undertake not to use your

telephone. Will that suit your wishes? The only alternative is a very unpleasant one in view of what has happened. We have definite information that you have been conveying information to the enemy, and that of course is a matter for which under ordinary circumstances, I have no choice but to put you under arrest. I do not want to do that in this case until we have gone a little further into the matter, so I am suggesting this as a middle course, that you should go out and have lunch and keep your appointment, and come down here again just after five.

A watch was placed outside De László's studio. Just in case.

At 5.30 p.m., De László returned and the questioning continued. He was asked about an erasure in his diary for 30 May 1917 and whether this might be connected with the letter he hotly denied he had sent to Geneva. His reply was that it would have concerned a sitter who had cancelled and this was his usual practice in such cases 'to keep my book tidy'. After further questions relating to diary entries that De László said related to other sitters or about people with whom he had lunched, Thomson launched into the use of the diplomatic bag, following a question about whether De László knew Mr van Swinderen, the Dutch Minister in London. De László admitted to having met him only once before the war, to having lunched with him, at van Swinderen's invitation, a couple of months before the interrogation, and to having invited him to attend a house party for his friends the Raemaekers. Asked how he had been able to persuade him to let him use the diplomatic bag on the basis of so casual an acquaintance, De László said that he never really knew it was the diplomatic bag. At the start of the war he had contacted Madame van Riemsdyk asking her to be his intermediary in Holland, but he did not know how her letters came and it was on her suggestion that he had gone to van Swinderen, and he had taken her letter to him personally. After that he had taken a couple personally, but usually he sent them by hand.

Thomson then announced, 'Now, I suppose you have gathered that we have been seeing some of your correspondence for some time.' De László said he had realised that, and Thomson immediately said, 'I am going to read you a letter in French, it is a French translation of a letter, because the original was not written in French. Then I will ask you whether you have received the letter. It was written to you at 3 Palace Gate.' The letter of 14 June was then read to him (the one that mentioned his report was 'of the highest importance').

De László's response was emphatic: 'I have never received that letter, it cannot have been addressed to me. I do not know who can have written it; nor have I ever written anything about those things.' Thomson then told him it was believed that he had used the bag rather more than five or six times and De László admitted that each envelope may have contained more than one letter, perhaps two or three. Thomson reiterated he meant more than five or six sendings, then suddenly announced, 'I think it is right to tell you that we have further information to this effect that in those letters you gave the exact date of the loss of English ships, the figures and statistics relative to the critical situation on account of the mines, and particularly the gossip about the King's view of the war.' This was material which, if correct, could lead to the death penalty, and De László immediately replied, 'I do not understand it; I never wrote anything concerning the war.' When pressed over whether he had written anything about peace, he said he may have mentioned to his brother that he hoped there would be peace, but stressed he had never written to anyone about the war.

De László was questioned briefly about his Jewish origins and stated that he had destroyed none of the letters he had received. Thomson then returned to the subject of his wishing to regain his Hungarian nationality, as he thought he might have said something with a view to impressing his fellow former nationals.

De László then returned (apparently) to the story he had told earlier about the Hungarian he had met at the start of the war. This time he named him as Sbenenyei [*sic*] and said he had actually been told not to meet him by Baron Forster, but had done so. The man had brought him various pieces he had received from Hungary – 'unpleasant things' – and asked him to write something for the Hungarian press in response. De László had written something which he thought would be published in the responsible newspapers, but instead it had appeared in some kind of cheap journal or pamphlet. He certainly didn't think it implied a desire to get back his original nationality. Thomson also mentioned a letter to De László's sister, which he had written to her on the death of her son. This, he said, had impressed upon the censor the feeling that he was referring to Hungary as his home. De László denied the impression was intended.

Thomson then impressed upon De László the necessity, in time of war, to have the matters he had raised investigated, with which De László agreed. He again, however, denied having received the letter in question. They discussed Baron Forster and De László said that he had kept all his letters from him, but not copies of his letters to him, but that their contents could be deduced from the replies. In particular he referred to correspondence which had passed about meetings that his brother had had with Count Andrassy, leader of the Hungarian opposition in Parliament and president of the Art Society, about the naturalisation. Fortunately his brother had kept a copy of a letter he had received two years before the war talking about British naturalisation, which had convinced him that Andrassy was genuine. Having presumably seen the copied correspondence from MI5 and the Special Section, Thomson pointed out that this letter must have come through the diplomatic bag. De László responded that he couldn't say because it was only recently that he had started keeping the *couverts* (envelopes).

Thomson returned to the delicacy of his position: 'You were naturalized after the beginning of the war, yet, when you ought to have had everything smooth and open, you are sending letters clandestinely through the Legation Bag.' Expressing his regret, De László solemnly promised that they would never find any letters either sent or received by him about the war. When asked whether it had ever occurred to him that he was in breach of the censorship law, he said it had never occurred to him until he had heard van Swinderen discussing it on the phone in August 1916, and since then he had not sent anything by that route.

Thomson then produced a letter dated 24 July 1917 from Madame van Riemsdyk to Mrs De László, in which she said that she was sending it by 'the ordinary route'. Didn't this imply that she was using another route up to that time? De László was adamant that he had not sent anything out by that route, and said that he had promised as much to the Attorney General on meeting him. When he discovered Madame van Riemsdyk was still using the bag to send items to him, he had written to her asking her not to, and had later asked his wife to do the same thing. He was quite sure that of the five or six letters that had gone out through the bag, all had gone before August 1916.

Thomson then asked De László about a set of family photographs he had sent to Hungary. De László said it was probable they had gone via the legation but didn't remember. Thomson pointed out that the censorship did not allow such things to go through the ordinary post, so they must have gone through the bag to Holland. There was an acknowledgement of receipt of these photos dated 5 August 1917, so surely they must have gone out quite recently? De László fell back on what appears to have been a usual tactic, changing the subject by saying, 'I received photographs of my people – snapshots of the family', which must have come to him via the embassy the previous year.

Quite why Thomson should have left it there we don't know, but he suddenly announced that De László could return to Datchet and that the authorities would let him know when he would next be required. No doubt MI5 continued to have him watched and his mail intercepted.

The man heading the MI5 investigation at this time was Major Ernest St George Anson, an officer in the regular army of some experience. Born in 1874 and educated at Clifton College, he had seen extensive service during the Boer War, fighting in the Relief of Ladysmith, at Colenso, Spion Kop, the Tugela Heights, Pieters Hill and Laing's Nek. He had been adjutant of the 3rd Battalion of the East Surreys, and had qualifications . in gymnastics, musketry, signalling, cycling and supply. He also spoke French. Having gone to France in January 1915, he was presumably wounded or taken sick at the front and, after a period of recuperation, posted to MI5 in December 1915. He remained in G2 Section (investigation of the bona fides of persons) until December 1919. Whilst senior officers and experienced lawyers sat in on the interrogations, Anson was the man who co-ordinated things behind the scenes. He would have decided the priorities for the investigators, examined new evidence as it came in, and discussed it with Vernon Kell, who had the delicate job of deciding what action to take over a man with so many high-level connections. Basil Thomson, in the meantime, was making more public enquiries among people who had had their portraits painted over the previous couple of years or who knew De László personally.

Thomson contacted various of De László's sitters and obtained a statement from Mrs Wanda Muller regarding his behaviour during the painting of her portrait:

I first went to Mr De László to have my picture painted about September 1915, but the first attempt was a failure. He then wrote to me asking to postpone the sittings for a month or so, as he had several officers to paint who were going to the war.

In October 1915 he started on a second canvas as he was not satisfied with what he had already done, but after one sitting which also failed to please him, he began a third picture.

I had met Mr De László in this country before going to Hungary in 1913 and thought he seemed intelligent with a gift for languages. He took a great interest in politics especially of course in those of his own country Hungary.

The first sitting for the third canvas took place before the end of October, and during the course of the sittings he talked a great deal about Hungary.

At one of the sittings he remarked on British politics and discussed the British policy with regard to Roumania. He criticised the action of the government on this question and also a good deal else in the country, from the point of view of a Hungarian. At another sitting he told me he hated the Servians [sic] and that he sincerely hoped that they would soon be wiped off the earth. I replied that it was impossible to admire all our allies equally and it was certainly not the moment to criticise them publicly whatever one's own private opinions might be. It was obvious that he hated the Russians with the intense hatred of a Hungarian. In the end I told him that we had better not discuss politics as there was such flat disagreement between us. He looked upon everything from a Hungarian point of view and I from an English. I cannot remember any details of the conversation I had with Mr De László, but the impression he gave me was that his sympathies were still Hungarian to the backbone. He seemed to me to wish to have it both ways, to retain the advantages of living in England, and when the war came, he could not make up his mind to give up his Hungarian sympathies.

His visits to the different Courts of Europe had obviously turned his head, and he expressed the greatest admiration for the 'Divine William' and the King of Greece. On my expressing strong dissent from all his views in regard to the Emperor he exclaimed 'Well, anyhow, that is what I think, and you will probably tell everyone that I am a pro-German.' As a matter of fact he did not give me the impression of being a pro-German, but rather what he is, a Hungarian to the backbone, and I did not regard him as loyal Englishman.

Mr László was very indiscreet. He used to tell me what Mr Austen Chamberlain, and Mr Fisher (Lord Fisher's son) and others had told him, but I am unable to remember any details of the conversations. I remember in particular Mr László telling me that he had a conversation on military matters with Major (blanked in original) an officer employed at the War Office. I was very disagreeably impressed at the time, though the conversation may not have been of much importance, as Mr László has told me himself that he sent letters in the Dutch Bag to friends in Hungary. In fact I was so disturbed that I went so far as to ask a mutual friend to warn Major (blanked in original) against talking so openly to Mr De László, as he was to all intents and purposes an enemy alien, and I did not regard him as a loyal British Subject.

Another unnamed sitter (probably Henry Vincent Higgins, a prominent solicitor) was presumably, from the content of the report, someone Thomson briefed in advance. A report dated 8 August 1917 read:

After some time L said suddenly 'I am tired of pictures so let us talk about the war.' He then said that England had a glorious opportunity now of making peace. As long as the Russian Empire was intact, she was in great danger, because, with Constantinople and Persia, the Russians would cut her off from her eastern possessions. Now this danger passed, England stood victorious, and could accomplish all her ends. As to America, they did not intend to fight at all. Their object was merely to awaken a military spirit against the time they would have to fight against Mexico and Japan. Informant said these sentiments might have come from mouth of Bernstorff. It struck informant that L was delivering a series of sentiments put into his mouth for propaganda, because he invariably lacked the knowledge to combat arguments on the other side, and did not attempt to do so. It struck him that L was very vain of his accomplishments as a diplomatist and also very shallow, like his pictures.

Informant also tried more than once to bring the conversation round to Holland, and asked L whether he had any friends there, but he drew a blank every time. L did not deny knowing people but he appeared uninterested and uncommunicative.

Thomson also produced a report from another sitter, summarised in the evidence file, a lady whose husband, a civil servant, had reported:

Wife was sitting for L about two years ago (so late summer 1915). L was incessantly talking politics, and supporting the usual Hungarian view that Serbia ought to be wiped out of existence, and that the Russians were the natural enemies of mankind. His political bias was so marked, that at last his sitter had to request that he should not talk politics. It transpired that L was sending letters through the Dutch Legation bag, and (the sitter's husband) thought it right to convey an unofficial warning, both to Mr Van Swinderen and to L, that this was contrary to the Regulations.

On 29 August, De László was again summoned to Scotland Yard, this time for an interrogation regarding the contents of some of his correspondence. The interview was conducted by Basil Thomson, with Vernon Kell sitting in for the first time, and another MI5 officer, Captain Sir Lindsey Smith, in attendance. Smith had only joined MI5 in June 1917, but he had had a formidable legal career,

entering Middle Temple in 1889 and getting a first-class scholarship in Common and Criminal Law in1892. He was called to the
Bar the same year. He had had long colonial service as president of
HM Court of Appeal in East Africa between 1904 and 1909, and as
a judge in the Supreme Court, China and Korea. In his youth he
had been a useful rugby player for Surrey and the Barbarians.

Presumably this was held in Thomson's office where,
by design, the interviewee was seated in a lower chair than his
interviewer, which was supposed to put him in an inferior position and make lying harder.

Thomson, who fancied himself as a master interrogator,
started with some innocuous questions:

ACC: I wanted to see you today on matters that have arisen
      through examination of your papers, because there are
      some things only you can explain. You know a certain
      Comte de Soissons?

PAL: Comte de Soissons is an art critic and was introduced to
      me by a colleague. He has been in my studio four or five
      times and is, I think, rather a fool. When he last dined
      with me I had Mr Laughlin from the American Embassy
      and his wife and other guests with me, and he more or
      less insulted him. I have never seen the man since.

ACC There is among your papers a letter from your brother-
      in-law dated 17th August 1914.

PAL: Mr Kremer?

ACC No, Mr Guinness (letter read to him). This implies you
      put down the origin of the war to the Russians rather
      than the Germans.

PAL Yes, he came very often, and I remember we had a
      conversation and I said that there was always unrest
      amongst the Russians and that possibly the Russians
      were more or less to blame.

ACC   I think you have always since the outbreak of the war
       been subject to 'Russo-phobia'?

PAL   I do not know. In 1848 the Hungarians fought for their
       independence against Austria and Austria was beaten.
       Then at the last moment, Austria united with Russia and
       behaved very badly towards them afterwards.

ACC   Since the war began it has been the current view
       throughout Hungary that Russia was responsible for
       the war.

PAL   Well, I do not know much about that.

ACC   What was Baron Forster's view?

PAL   I assure you, Sir, that I have never had any political
       conversation with Forster. My connection with Forster is
       absolutely on an artistic footing.

ACC   Yes, but we know from various things that your view since
       the beginning of the war has been that the Russians were
       largely responsible for it. You said so to Mr Guinness.

PAL   Well, I said it to him, but it is very difficult to say that
       it is my view because one reads so much and we talk on
       the war; I give my opinion, but it cannot be taken as a
       serious matter.

ACC   No, there is nothing serious about it, I just wanted to get
       at your views.

PAL   I must have said that. We were probably having an
       argument and I naturally took the opposite view.

ACC   That is also the view of the official German party.
       The Kaiser has been good enough to tell us more than once.

PAL   Is that so? I remember once when I was invited to
       Wilhelmshaven I was very annoyed with the Kaiser.
       There was a big exhibition at Berlin arranged by
       Count Sechendorff who was a great friend of mine.
       There was one picture there, which is now in the
       National Gallery, by Reynolds, which the Kaiser

loved, and he wanted me to paint a full-sized portrait of himself in the same position. I was very annoyed with him because he wanted me to paint in the corner of the picture some emblems – the German Imperial Crown. I said 'What is the German Imperial Crown?' He was very annoyed at my saying that and said 'You ought to know better than to ask such a question. The German Imperial Crown is in Vienna and should have come to us after 1866, and of course you Hungarians do not like these things because you do not like the Germans at all.'

ACC   I suppose you preserve the photographs and telegrams with regard to the Kaiser from an historic point of view?

PAL   Yes.

ACC   That was one of the studies, was it not (photograph shown)?

PAL   Yes.

ACC   I want to run rapidly through one or two little points. You corresponded with and gave money to, I think, three young Hungarians. (Names mentioned.)

PAL   De Weress is a young gentleman of very good family from the south of Hungary. He came here to study, and when the *Lusitania* was sunk, the Hungarians, I understood from the American Ambassador, were interned and he with them, but before that he had written asking if I would see him, which I did. I saw he was a very nice man and we became friends. Through him I met a man named the Revd. Hankinson who was responsible for him. He is a Unitarian who had been in Hungary. Hankinson is engaged to Mrs Hill who is a niece of my wife.

ACC   Did you know De Weress was mixed up with the man named Rawson?

PAL Yes, I know that too. Weress came to me several times
     in great distress saying how badly he had been treated
     by Mr Hankinson. Hankinson annoyed him very much,
     but I always told him he must bear it because after all
     the man had been very nice to him. He met a lady at
     Hankinson's house and she brought him to that man
     Rawson and he became absolutely obsessed by Rawson.

ACC Then you befriended him at Alexandra Palace by
     sending him Hungarian newspapers.

PAL Yes, I received them through Louis Feldmann who was
     secretary of the Hungarian Society. When the war broke
     out he asked if I could help the Hungarians.

ACC Was this before or after war had started?

PAL Immediately after. Then I helped them. I think I gave
     altogether £60.00. Weress told me about Czeizner and
     then I introduced Czeizner to Hankinson. Then Weress
     was interned. I would like to tell you how I came to
     visit the Concentration Camp. Weress and my niece
     met in my house. I always implored him not to go to
     Rawson. Before he was interned his parents were dining
     with us and I called him up to my room and asked him
     again to leave off these things. Then I heard through
     the girl that the money his parents were sending him
     was getting more and more reduced and that some law
     had been made in Hungary that he could only have a
     certain amount. I said to him 'Weress, do not go to that
     man and I will give you £20 as I hear you are in need of
     money.' He was very pleased and promised me not to
     go there again and I said 'If you are in need of money
     I will give you more.' The next morning we heard he
     was interned, so my wife, my niece and myself went to
     see him. To our great astonishment Weissner told us
     that Weress had been removed to the Isle of Man. Then

I made the acquaintance of Weissner and liked him very much and helped him.

ACC   You subscribed also anonymously to the Council of Loyal British Subjects of German and Hungarian birth?

PAL   Yes. I did that almost against my will. I had no connection with them, but a man came to me one day with his card and asked for money, and I said, I cannot help you, as I give so much to other charities; but I will give you £10 and no more.

ACC   You also subscribed to Sokobow, I think. We have a letter from him from the Regent Palace Hotel.

PAL   It is an old friend who was twenty-five years British Embassy Chaplain. He is a pensioner who comes to our house and he asked me to help do something for the Jews, so I gave him £5 or £10.

ACC   I think you told me last time that your brother is in business in Pesth.

PAL   Yes.

ACC   And you told me he had seen Count Andrassy?

PAL   Yes, once or twice as I understand from his letters.

ACC   Why should he have visited him?

PAL   I understand from his letter he was called by Count Andrassy who knows he is my brother, because I understood from the letter from Forster that he was not quite on my side. They called a meeting, of which Forster was actually the president, but he wrote very little about it. He only mentioned it in the first letter: the one that came through Switzerland. Count Andrassy said 'We cannot decide on taking down his pictures until we hear from him that he only naturalised because war broke out.' Forster and Andrassy are great friends. He evidently invited my brother to give him some explanation as to his naturalisation, for my brother wrote and said 'Luckily enough I have found a letter I received from you in which you speak of your naturalisation.' My brother showed him this letter showing that I had had the idea for a long time: Baron Forster must have told him the same thing for when I painted him in 1913 I told him about it and he said to me then 'I think anyone in your position would do the same thing.'

ACC Now, we have a good deal of experience here in the matter of naturalisation and of course you know that certain people, Baron Schroeder, for instance, were naturalised let us put it, for technical reasons. It was a convenience for them, and perhaps to other people, that they should be described as British subjects.

PAL When I applied for naturalisation I never thought of war, then war broke out and I did not think there would be any difficulty. On the second or third day we saw a placard that all Germans not naturalised had to be registered or something of the kind. I said to my wife 'It is very annoying; probably it will come in to Austria-Hungary too.' When I saw that I wrote immediately to Mr McKenna whom I met once, asking why I had not yet received my papers, and I got my naturalisation two or three days later.

ACC You never did register as an enemy alien?

PAL No.

ACC When were you actually naturalised?

PAL On the 29th August.

ACC That was after the date of the Austrian declaration of war. Then when did you hear that this naturalisation had been looked at in a hostile way in Buda-Pesth?

PAL When a man came and visited me in September bringing me a letter of introduction from an old friend of mine. Through that letter I received him and then he went home to Hungary and made trouble, because it came out in the papers that I was naturalised. That was about the end of September 1914 that he took the news to Hungary that I had been naturalised.

ACC   On the 19th October you received a letter from Madame Van Riemsdyk saying 'Your Hungarian friend has not been to see us so far?' Was that the same man?

PAL   Yes, it must have been. He said he would probably stay in Holland, and I said 'If you go there you can call on the van Riemsdyks.'

ACC   It was a great shock for you at first that this attack had been made on you in Hungary?

PAL   It was a very nasty attack. I wrote in that pamphlet that I had always done honour to my native land in the past, and my colleagues ought to have had the consideration to ask me first how I was naturalised.

ACC   The point at issue was really this, that there was their country actually at war, or on the eve of war, and that one of their countrymen suddenly divested himself of his nationality.

PAL   But I'm a human being, and it took me two years to decide.

ACC   What I meant was that the difference between you and the Hungarians was one which there was no getting over, for you cannot explain away to the Hungarians the fact that you did become a British subject.

PAL   I wrote to Forster and to my brother saying I was going to be naturalised. I love to be English. I want to live in a big world where all art is centralised and where my children were born.

ACC   You had no interest in Hungary: that is what you wanted to convey to them.

PAL   I was interested in Hungary and I shall always be very grateful for what I have received there. I had all the honour in Hungary that a man can have.

ACC   But I suppose you said to yourself when you got
       naturalised, 'I have got all these honours and
       distinctions in Hungary, they must all go.'

PAL   No, I never thought of that.

ACC   I will read you what purports to be a translation of a
       cutting from 'The Star' dated November 17th 1914
       (this was read to him).

The Star was a London newspaper and the letter in question,
which had been discovered by MI5 early in its investigation
(and which may have prompted its original interest) read:

> My hand trembles when I think in how serious an hour I write
> these lines, and I fear that while I sit quietly here at my table and
> write, already perhaps many brave people will have lost their lives on
> account of the predatory SERVIAN nation. Another serious thing
> has also happened, I have signed the papers relating to English citi-
> zenship and for three weeks past have been a BRITISH SUBJECT.
> The customary witnesses who testified that for five years they
> had known me as a 'Gentleman' were my friends the members
> of Parliament Lord Balfour, Lee, Lord Devonport and Guinness.
> It has cost me a severe mental conflict, but on account of my five
> sons I had to do it.

De László responded:

PAL   It is all absolute nonsense what they are saying there. I keep
       those papers because so many ridiculous things have been
       written. I never wrote that letter. [Next to this someone had
       added a pencil note: 'I think he did HO paper p 150'.]

ACC   This is said to be a letter received by your relations in
       Buda-Pesth. Is it not possible that this is one of the
       letters your brother showed to Count Andrassy?

PAL   No, I do not think so; that letter was dated in 1912.

ACC How could they have got these details about your sureties? Would they have forged those, and also about your five sons, to damage you?

PAL   They did many things like that, but I could not have written that letter to him, because – I must come back now to the unfortunate fact that I sent some letters through the Dutch Legation – I would not have dared to write a letter like that, for someone would probably have seen it and gone home and told lies about it.

My idea was to keep these things to how my native people behaved so badly and to show them how unjust they were.

ACC In fact you were keeping them to rehabilitate yourself with the Hungarians after the war. Why should your brother have gone to see Count Andrassy unless it was to rehabilitate yourself with the Hungarians?

PAL   Certainly he did it for that, because the outcry was that I did it when the war broke out, and they would not believe I thought of it before the war.

ACC Quite so, but the fact would remain that you had before the war wished to wash your hands of the Hungarians.

PAL   It never came into my head.

ACC Did you never wish to do that?

PAL   I had only one idea, which I still have, and that was to show them that I did not do it during the war. If I had, they would have been quite right to speak of me as they did.

ACC As a matter of fact you did not want to wash your hands of any country; is that so?

PAL   Yes.

ACC When you became naturalised you took a solemn oath of allegiance and my point is that you had a divided allegiance; you wanted to get the advantages of being a naturalised British subject and you took the oath of allegiance, but in your heart you made reserves.

You did not want to stand badly with the Hungarians.

PAL   No, it was simply a point of honour; I never did anything wrong in my life. A long time before I got married I did think of living in Hungary and I built a beautiful home there which still stands. Now for four years I have had the intention of building a house there [*sic*]. I sold my house in Hungary.

ACC   Mr László, did you write your own biography in *Who's Who*?

PAL   Yes, I was asked various questions when I came to live in England and they write to me every year and add to it.

ACC   So you did not get rid of your Hungarian status when you assumed British nationality?

PAL   No, I have a legal right to my name.

ACC   I am not disputing your right, but only suggesting that you were trying to keep a foot in both countries.

PAL   The title is equal to that of a British Baron which gives the children the right to keep the name forever. I cannot lose that.

ACC   But the Buda-Pesth paper suggests that this should be done.

PAL   I do not think that can be.

ACC   You do not want that done?

PAL   Well, I never thought of it.

ACC   Many British holders of foreign titles have divested themselves of them.

PAL   If it is necessary I am willing to do that.

ACC   It is not a question of that; I am trying to get at what your mind is.

PAL   My point is that I got the honour in an honourable way through my work.

ACC But when the Buda-Pesth paper said it should be taken away you thought it better for your brother to see Count Andrassy.

PAL No, because Count Andrassy had I know a very great feeling for me, for he bought my very first picture from me when I was twenty. I only know what my brother wrote to me.

ACC Bearing on that, I should rather like to call your attention to a series of newspaper cuttings that have been found. They do not refer, as one would expect, to art or Hungarian politics, but they do refer to air raids, sinking of a cruiser, revolution in Russia, trouble in Greece, peace pamphlets etc. It is curious that this little hoard should be made of things that are hostile to this country. I want to know why they were kept.

PAL You mean I kept these papers on purpose?

ACC Yes, I suggest it. They were in the interests of Hungary and against the interest of this country.

PAL I remember two or three articles which appeared in the "Globe" in favour of Hungary.

A packet of documents discovered at his Datchet home was then shown to him.

PAL I know who brought me that (uklenftucke zum Ariegsausbruch) it was old Professor Haeckler.

ACC Who is Professor Haeckler?

PAL He was at the British Embassy in Vienna for about twenty-five years, when I lived in Vienna, which was only for a year and a half.

ACC Here is a nice little collection which it would interest me to know how you got and why. [Thomson seems to have been indicating the left-wing British pacifist documents such as National Labour Press.]

PAL   I never bought these things: they were brought to me by
       Professor Haeckler. He brought me some and I told him
       not to bring me any more.

ACC   Where is he now?

PAL   He lives at Barnet. He is British born, and comes to my
       house very frequently.

ACC   Is he a Socialist?

PAL   No.

ACC   But he goes to these meetings.

PAL   I give you my word I have never read these. They were
       all brought to me by that old man and when we went
       into the country they were packed up together.

ACC   Why did you keep them?

PAL   They were packed up there.

ACC   But some were found at Datchet.

PAL   They must have been sent to me.

ACC   Who sends them?

PAL   I am engaged with that Company.

ACC   The cuttings that are sent by a company are always clear cut
       at the edges and stuck on a paper, like these, but the cuttings
       I am referring to are not; they have been cut out by yourself.

PAL   I remember now that one or two papers have been sent
       to me to read and to my wife by my sister-in-law, Miss
       Guinness. There is a pamphlet here by a Unitarian
       Bishop. Mr Hankinson wrote to me lately asking me to
       help with money a Hungarian lady and he sent me these
       pamphlets, which I never read.

ACC   Why did you keep that? ('Pacifism in England –
       Through German Eyes'.)

PAL   I do not know.

ACC   You are a pacifist are you not?

PAL   I am not a pacifist, but I would like Hungary to become
       absolutely independent out of this war.

ACC   I know from what people who have sat for you have told
      me what you say. Shall I give you an instance?

PAL   Please.

ACC   One particular one was about the coming in of America,
      that it was futile to count on America, that America was
      only using this war as an excuse to arm against Japan and
      Mexico; they did not mean or would not provide any real
      help. That I know you said, and I suppose you meant it.

PAL   I am in an awful position in my studio. I see so many
      people and one talks.

ACC   I will give you a little more. That it was of supreme
      moment to Great Britain to make peace at this moment:
      that she had got all she wanted and that it was of supreme
      moment that she should make peace. If the Russians had
      stood firm they would have come in like a wedge between
      her and her eastern powers. Did you say that or not?

PAL   If you have heard it: probably there was some talk of war.

ACC   This was a talk you introduced.

PAL   I had a talk with Colonel Repington (the noted war
      correspondent for *The Times*) and we lunched at the
      Ritz Hotel with two ladies and talked about the war.

ACC   This was not Colonel Repington. The point is, will you
      deny that you ever said words to that effect – that this
      was the moment to make peace?

PAL   That I never said, but I remember saying once to
      someone that whatever happens, no nation will come
      out morally so great and well as England.

ACC   Do you deny ever saying to anybody that this was the
      moment for England to make peace?

PAL   I never remember saying that.

ACC   Could you have said it?

PAL   No, I will give you my word of honour that I never said
      any such thing.

ACC I am afraid that your memory is a little defective on
     that point. That is not so material, it was only that
     I wanted to test your memory, and I want to test your
     memory in one respect. There are a number of people
     who quite genuinely think that from a political point
     of view it would be best to make peace, but it had a
     peculiar bearing in your case for reasons that you have
     already gathered, that we have reason to think that your
     allegiance is divided between the two countries.

PAL You cannot expect it from me; I can prove it through
     my friends in France that it is impossible for me to go
     back; on the other hand, I cannot suddenly turn my
     back on a country or curse it, or anything like that.
     It was not Hungary who caused the war; it is of no
     interest to her; her one interest would be to become
     free of Austria.

ACC But to one who loves both countries, reconciliation
     between the two would be most agreeable.

PAL I would be very happy if Hungary would make friends.
     (Paper shown him)

PAL Professor Haeckler gave me that: he is a very strange
     old gentleman. He was a great friend of the Duke of
     Teck and gave lessons to his children. He goes to all
     kinds of meetings. I would like to give an explanation
     of the German papers. Old Baron Schleintz lived in
     this country; he was in charge for Leipsic to write what
     happens on art matters. He was to write the biography
     of British Artists and one day he came to me and said
     'I have been asked to write your life', so I had to give
     him all material. He died nearly two years ago and
     the old Baroness and an old Fraulein live alone; we
     visit them sometimes, and I got my German papers
     from there.

ACC Where did you get the Blue Book on the papers found in
     the possession of Archibald – the man who was caught
     at Falmouth carrying papers?

PAL I do not know, but I expect Professor Haeckler gave me
     that too.

ACC Do you receive any Hungarian papers from your relatives?

PAL No, never.

ACC Did you know Mr Arthur Diosy?

PAL I met him once in my life, many years ago. I was never
     a member of the Hungarian Society here, or of the
     Austrian, but once I went to a concert with my wife and
     we met him, but I do not believe I have seen him since,
     and he sent me a book he wrote.

ACC Now, I want to go rapidly through another matter.
     Your transmission of funds to your mother. You gave
     an explanation about the £200, intended to be sent
     through Baron Mayendorff. The police officer made a
     report that you said this was to be part of the £1,000
     that Mayendorff owed you for a picture, but you
     explained afterwards that you had given him a cheque.
     Was that the only amount that you sent your mother?

PAL No, I sent her more money, but not through him.

ACC When you sent this other money was it before or after
     June of this year?

PAL I must have sent the last money in June or July last year.

ACC Nothing since then?

PAL No.

ACC When you saw Sir Charles Mathews on the subject of
     this money did you tell him you had sent any money
     besides the £200?

PAL Yes.

ACC He says 'No'.

PAL He knew about it.

ACC   Did you tell him you had sent it through the Dutch
      Legation Bag?

PAL   I never sent money that way.

ACC   How did you do it?

PAL   It was always done through my bank.

ACC   You sent £400 to Blydenstein, but that did not go from
      the bank, apparently. We have here a list of the amounts,
      making a total of £2,100 up to the 21st November 1915.
      Then we come to 1916; there was the £200 to Mayendorff:
      there was also £400 paid to Blydenstein, what was that?

PAL   Madame van Riemsdyk wrote to me and I sent a letter
      to the London and Counties Bank asking them to send
      so much to Madame van Riemsdyk; that was done
      constantly. One day I had a letter from Madame van
      Riemsdyk in which she said there were complications
      with regard to getting the money, and I said 'Would it
      not be wiser for me to write to Blydenstein and he sends
      it straight through to your bank in The Hague?', and I
      did that once: my niece married and I sent her some
      money. After that, Madame van Riemsdyk wrote to me
      'Please do not send more money through Blydenstein
      until you do not hear from me again.' I think that was
      the time my brother-in-law told me that I ought to
      have permission.

ACC   Last March you sent through the National Foreign
      Securities £500 – what was that for?

PAL   They are shares that I bought through my broker.

ACC   There is a letter to Mayendorff. (Letter read to him
      as follows: '29th October 1916. My dear good friend,
      I congratulate you on the good news. We have had
      reason to foresee that the question will turn out badly
      for the enemies (les adversaires). I see with what joy you
      have learnt the good news.') What was the news?

PAL   I really do not know what he meant by that.

ACC   That is your cheque.

PAL   Yes.

ACC   Do you know what Baron Mayendorff's position is as
       regards the revolution? From conversation with him
       what would you take him to be, for the New Regime or
       the Old Regime?

PAL   That I cannot say.

ACC   Now I want to go back to what we talked about last
       time – sending letters through the bag. Have you
       refreshed your memory at all as to the number of letters
       you sent.

PAL   I have asked Miss Lundquist, my wife's maid who took
       the letters for me to Mr van Swinderen. I just said to her,
       'Will you tell me how many letters you have taken to the
       Dutch Legation', and she said to me 'About four or five'.

ACC   Did you ever hand them over yourself?

PAL   Yes, once or twice. The very first and I think the very last
       one in August last year.

ACC   Did you have had [sic] them coming through the bag
       coming the other way quite recently?

PAL   Yes. Immediately after I saw the Director of Public
       Prosecutions I wrote to Madame van Riemsdyk, and I
       think one or two letters came through the bag afterwards.
       Since August last year there have been no letters from me,
       and I have seen van Swinderen only once.

ACC   Beyond the hint that he gave on the telephone, did he
       ever suggest to you that it was irregular for your letters
       to go that way?

PAL   No, he never said it.

ACC   You remember you told me last time that your
       correspondence with Forster probably went by that
       means as far as you could remember.

PAL One letter I got from Switzerland, but there must have been one or two letters which went to Madame van Riemsdyk.

ACC But you told me that last time and you also said you had kept all Forster's letters.

PAL Yes, I have them all.

ACC We cannot find them. Could you lay your hands on them at lunchtime and let us have them?

PAL Certainly.

ACC I did put this question to you last time, but I will put it to you again. I quite understand that Madame van Riemsdyk found it convenient to send her letters via the Foreign Office, but I do not understand now why you adopted that method. Why should you have gone to the trouble of sending a maid all the way to Green Street, when she could have dropped the letters into the pillar box at the corner of the street?

PAL I never thought about it really.

ACC But why did you do it? – it was not a question of postage which deterred you. You were sending letters through the post to Madame van Riemsdyk at the same time, and some went through the Legation Bag.

PAL All my letters went straight to her with the exception of those five or six times when they went through van Swinderen. Madame van Riemsdyk made me the offer because she knew how anxious I always am to hear from my people.

ACC My point is that you did not do it every time.

PAL I probably did not want to annoy him so often.

ACC You said to me last time that you had been in communication with Baron Forster who is an enemy, a Hungarian, and you then admit to me that your letters to Baron Forster probably went through this means, but at the same time Madame van Riemsdyk, you tell me, had asked you to do this, and yet at the same time you were sending ordinary letters through the post which were not addressed to Baron Forster.

PAL   I have sent all my letters straight with the exception of five or six times.

ACC   Was it not because you thought the Censor might stop them?

PAL   No.

ACC   Then why not send them by post?

PAL   Because it was an easier and quicker way.

ACC   But it involves a criminal charge.

PAL   I was not thinking of that.

ACC   The point is that you did send some by the ordinary route. I should have thought very little of it if you had had that request and from that point onwards had sent your letters through the Legation Bag, but you did not: you used the post for certain letters and others you sent through the bag. When you had to communicate with a Member of the Upper House in Hungary, a Member of Parliament for the Enemy, you did it secretly.

PAL   No, there was nothing secret in it at all.

ACC   But it is a secret way; we had not got access to the Dutch Bag. Who is Professor B?

PAL   That is the man I spoke to you about who took news of me to my family. I cannot remember his name.

ACC   Who is Dr R? Is that Dr Revess?

PAL   I have been told he was working here for years studying British law and constitution and Hankinson wrote to me to ask if I would help his wife.

ACC   Could Miss Lundquist have put a letter of her own into the bag?

PAL   No, my letters were in an envelope addressed to him.

ACC   I think really the point now is that we should like to see
      the Forster letters. There are a good many of your papers
      we can now return to you.

He was told he would be communicated with further.

Following the interview, Vernon Kell, in his capacity as head
of MI5 and a competent military authority, wrote a detailed
report on the case, along with his recommendation to the home
secretary that De László be interned immediately. After giving
a very brief resumé of De László's life and pointing out that he
had naturalised after the outbreak of the war, MI5 turned to the
meat of the matter:

He first came to the attention of MI5 in February 1915 by
reason of an intercepted telegram addressed to him to van
Riemsdyck, 8 Orange-straat, The Hague, on the 16th of that
month that ran as follows:

'Please forward amount to Laszlo rootos Uteza 28 and wire
Lamar postponing journey writing'

As this telegram apparently referred to the despatch of money
to a Hungarian subject at a Hungarian address, MI5 communicated with the Bath Police and requested them to obtain an
explanation from the sender.

When interviewed by the Bath Police de László stated that the
telegram merely requested a friend of his at The Hague to send
particulars to Hungary regarding the recent death of his mother.

Information was subsequently received from a reliable source
to the effect that de László was sending money from this country to his relatives in Hungary, and steps were taken to exercise
special supervision over his correspondence.

This special supervision soon brought to light the fact that
he was corresponding freely with his relatives, and with a
Baron Forster in Hungary through the medium of a Madame

van Riemsdyk in Holland. Nothing calling for special notice was, however, observed until November 1916 when a letter addressed to Madame van Riemsdyk was intercepted. This letter, which was subsequently sent to the Foreign Trade Department, disclosed the fact that he had sent some money to his relatives in Hungary with the aid of a friend in Madrid.

De László was, accordingly, interviewed by the Metropolitan Police, and, as will be seen from the accompanying copy of their report that the money sent from Madrid to his brother in Hungary had been despatched by Baron Mayendorff of the Russian Embassy in Madrid, and was part of a sum of £1,000 owed by Baron Mayendorff to him, De László, in respect of a portrait which he had painted. De László, at this interview, also admitted having sent money from this country to his brother in Hungary via Holland.

It is understood that the Director of Public Prosecutions, to whom the matter was reported, saw de László and cautioned him not to offend in this manner again.

On the 7th July 1917 we received a secret service report from Paris to the effect that the Austrian Services in Switzerland had been receiving information from a certain Madame 'G' in England; and shortly afterwards, on the 12th July, the French secret service reported that the Austrian Services in Switzerland were receiving information from a Dutch subject who, in turn, received by him from de László stated by them to be a person who moved in official English circles, and they asked us to make very careful enquiries about this man, and communicate the results to them.

On the 14th July an agent of Mr Basil Thomson succeeded in obtaining a copy of a translation of a letter written in the Hungarian language by a Hungarian representative in Switzerland to de László, together with the enclosure contained therein. It will be seen that in this letter de László is encouraged to hope that he will attain his desire to be re-admitted to Hungarian nationality, that he is thanked for the numerous and valuable reports which he has sent from England to Hungary since the war started, through the medium of some person in Holland, and that he is evidently regarded by the writer as a valuable and trustworthy Hungarian agent in this country. The writer has apparently taken such steps as lie within his power to ensure de László's re-admission to Hungarian nationality.

Immediate and exhaustive enquiries about de László himself, and the mysterious 'Madame G' were made but without any tangible results.

Meanwhile, however, it had transpired that on the 17th July, about midday, an Austrian officer, named Horn, who had escaped from Donington Hall, had called on de László asking for money. De László gave him £1, and failed to inform the police of Horn's call until 1.40 pm on 18th July – over 24 hours after he knew of it.

An interesting piece of evidence of de László's real sentiments had also fallen into the hands of Mr Basil Thomson. It took the form of a note made by a sitter to de László, a person of foreign origin who moves in diplomatic and court circles in London, early in 1915. It will be seen from this note, which was made because the sitter was so struck with de László's pro-Hungarian sentiments, that the painter displayed marked anti-British bias, violent hatred of the Serbians and the Russians, the greatest admiration of the Kaiser, and interest in military matters.

This sitter's impression of de László was subsequently cor-roborated by the Norwegian Minister.

Mr Basil Thomson is prepared to vouch for the reliability of his informant, and for the accuracy of the statements made.

On the 24th July 1917 another Paris report further stated that de László was principally concerned with pacifist propa-ganda and gave further information about 'Madame G'.

On the same day a letter from Madame van Riemsdyk, stating that she was forwarding something 'by the ordinary route' was intercepted.

It was clear from this letter that de László had been communicating with Madame van Riemsdyk by some channel other than the ordinary post.

On the 4th August our Rotterdam agent reported that Adrienne Riemsdyk was known to have acted as intermediary for correspondence with Austria.

On the 8th August 1917, Mr Basil Thomson obtained from an informant whom he sent to de László with instructions to talk nothing but art to him, the report, of which a copy is attached. The informant found it impossible to confine de László to art, for he insisted on talking politics, and, in addition to displaying his usual antipathy to Russia, contended the USA did not intend to fight, and that the present was a splendid opportunity for Great Britain to make peace.

On the 14th August further information was received from a most reliable source from a sitter, who is employed in the Output Department of the Ministry of Munitions (a well-known public man who does not wish to appear). This gentleman reports that when having his portrait painted by de László in August 1917 he was asked two questions:

What was the output of munitions at the present time?

What was the consumption per week in France?

Matters which de László must have known to be within his knowledge.

At this stage it was decided that, in view of de László's opportunities for obtaining confidential information (he has painted the portraits of many well-known people, including Admiral Beatty and Lord Harding), of the fact that he was undoubtedly in correspondence by some route not supervised by the Censor, and that reports to the effect that he was an active enemy agent were in our possession, it would be dangerous to risk further delay, even with the object of securing definite evidence of espionage by him.

In these circumstances on the 15th August his premises were searched, and he was arrested and taken to Scotland Yard for examination. The scrutiny of his papers revealed the following facts:

He is the son of a Jew tailor of Budapest, and has a brother named Marcell and two or three sisters in Hungary. He married Lucy Guinness of Dublin by whom he has five sons. His bank books and income tax returns show that his income is about £12,000 a year, and that he has about £32,000 invested in England and America.

In addition he has money in German and Austrian securities and an account with the Bodin Credit Anstalt Bank, Vienna, which he seems to have been able to draw upon until the end of November 1914. A letter from a relation dated 17th June 1916 assures him that his property in Vienna is safe in the bank.

Some light is thrown upon his naturalisation by a press-cutting from the 'Star' of November 1914, from which it appears that he had written to a Budapest newspaper to the effect that his naturalization had cost him 'a severe mental conflict', but that, on account of his five sons, he 'had to do it'. His sentiments may be deduced from the letter written to him by Count de Soissons on the 27th October 1916, which shows quite clearly that both the writer and the recipient are strongly pro-Hungarian in sentiment.

A letter from his brother-in-law, dated 17th August 1914 (Original which shows that de László blamed the Russians for the war and not the Kaiser).

Several other letters show that he corresponded with and helped with money and gifts, three young Hungarian prisoners of war, one of these, K de WERRES, was concerned with the notorious Rawson.

Other letters show that he subscribed to the Council of Loyal British Subjects of German and Hungarian birth, but took great care that his subscriptions should be anonymous.

The most important correspondence, however, appears to be that with Adrienne van Riemsdyk. A letter from her dated 19th October 1914 contains the following passages: 'Your Hungarian friend has not been to see us so far – perhaps he went straight through to Pest'....'Your two letters to Buda Pest have gone to Vienna by special courier.'

In October 1915, the same writer says, 'I had just sent you, through our Legation in London, a fat letter ... I am hereby sending a couple of letters I received this morning.'

Another letter from his brother in an enemy country, dated 17th June 1916, contains the passage ...'Your property in Vienna is still at the bank as it was before and you need not worry you will get it after the declaration of peace.'

A letter dated 1st February 1917, from 'Daisy' the daughter of Madame van Riemsdyk, contains the following passages ...'I have asked Ferdie Michiels who has returned to his post at the Dutch Legation, London to take charge of it, to see that it arrives safely into my hands ... he knows all about it. I have told him everything, and as he is very precise and an old friend I know he will do his best.' (It relates to a frontispiece for a book which de László was to draw for her, apparently.) This letter is important because it shows that, in addition to the Dutch Diplomatic Bag being used the legation personnel was also made use of for the transmission of de László's correspondence.

Another letter dated 9th February 1917, from Madame van Riemsdyk states ... 'I received your kind lines of January 2nd two days ago and forwarded your letters to Baron Forster and the Bishop. I have just received the enclosed letter for you, and I hope it will reach you safely.'

Three other letters are attached which, though written from The Hague, were posted in London with English stamps, and must have travelled to London by Diplomatic Bag. These letters are dated 21st February, 27th April and 22nd May respectively.

Another letter from de László's brother, postmarked London July 23rd 1917, and containing the passage 'I have not received the £200 mentioned via Switzerland. You ought to enquire where they have got stuck.' This letter must also have arrived in this country by a similar route, and it indicates, in addition that de László was still apparently sending money to his brother in June 1917.

Not content with his channel of communication through Holland, de László evidently approached a Mr [Mrs was written in the original but amended to Mr] Winthrop Bowen, resident in New York, with a suggestion that she [*sic*] should act as an intermediary or him, for a letter from her [*sic*] dated 15th January 1915 which contains the following passages … 'yes, by all means send me any letters you wish me to forward to the continent of Europe' was found.

A cheque, and a letter from Baron de Mayendorff of the Russian Embassy in Madrid, were also found, and these documents clearly show that de László's explanation to the Police about the money which he endeavoured to send to his brother through Madrid was untrue. To the Police he stated that the money was part of a sum of £1000 which the Baron owed him, whereas it is evident that he drew a cheque in favour of the Baron to place him in funds for the transmission of the sum of £200 to his brother.

Copies of the reports of the interrogation of de László at New Scotland Yard are attached. It will be seen from these reports that he admitted to assisting the escaped prisoner of war Horn, and gave a somewhat unconvincing reason for having done so.

He twice stated that he had no friends in Spain, and no correspondence with them, and he only admitted the Mayendorff correspondence when pressed.

He first of all admitted to having sent 'five or six letters through the Dutch bag at the request of Madame van Riemsdyk, the last having been sent in August 1916, and all of them having been family letters'.

This he subsequently contradicted by admitting that he had corresponded with one Baron Forster, a member of the Upper House in Austria through the Dutch Bag. He admitted to having sent about seven letters to Baron Forster through the bag, but it seems highly probable that all the Forster letters, which from the replies we have seen must have been far more numerous, were sent through the bag.

He admitted also that he frequently wrote to Holland and to Hungary via the ordinary post, an admission which appears to be very significant. He admitted that the cheque for his brother had been taken by Mayendorff to Madrid, and denied having given the explanation recorded in the Police report of the 22nd February 1915, that the £200 was part of the £1000 owed him by Mayendorff. This denial cannot be believed, for the Police officer who reported it knew nothing of de László or his connection with Mayendorff.

He admitted having written a letter to Hungary explaining and excusing his change of nationality, and gave a very half-hearted denial of his alleged idea of resuming Hungarian nationality after the war – 'I do not believe I have.'

He volunteered what appears to be the significant information that his brother, an Austrian Jew tailor, has seen, on at least three occasions, Count Andrassy, the then Austrian Premier. De László stated that it was in connection with his naturalization in England, but it may well have been in connection with other matters of far greater importance to Hungary at the present time. He also admitted that he probably sent four small photographs out through the Dutch bag, photographs that were acknowledged so recently as 5th August 1917. It seems highly probable, therefore, that his statement that his correspondence through the Dutch Bag ceased in August 1916 is untrue. It should also be noted that when questioned as to the number of letters which he had sent through the bag he admitted that certain envelopes might have contained two or three letters each.

Finally, on the 22nd August 1917, Mr Basil Thomson furnished a further report containing information submitted to him by a sitter to de László respecting the latter's propensity for talking politics in a strongly pro-Hungarian and anti-Ally strain.

At this stage of the case the question whether de László should be prosecuted for the breaches of the Defence of the Realm Regulations which he had committed was very carefully considered in consultation with the Director of Public Prosecutions, but it was decided that the actual offences were, in themselves, comparatively insignificant when compared to the other, and infinitely more serious offence which he was very strongly suspected of having committed, and it was essential in the interests of public safety that de László should be interned for the duration of the war.

To sum up:

It is clearly established that de László is a person of hostile origin who for some reason, probably connected to his position in artistic circles in this country became a naturalized British subject after the outbreak of war. Hearing soon afterwards that he was being bitterly assailed for this in Hungary he deemed it desirable to write an apologia which appeared in a Hungarian newspaper within a few months of the naturalization.

It is also clear that he is a person of hostile associations. He has corresponded freely, not only with members of his own family in Hungary, but also with a member of the Hungarian Upper House, he has sent large sums of money to his family in Hungary, he has assisted an escaped prisoner of war with money, and he has corresponded with, sent money to, and visited interned Hungarians in this country.

The reports which have been submitted by sitters, and the contents of letters which were found when his premises were searched leave no room for doubt that he is strongly pro-Hungarian in sentiment, and that whenever a suitable opportunity has occurred he has indulged in pro-Hungarian, anti-Russian and anti-Ally peace propaganda.

His prevarications on the subject of the despatch of money to Hungary, and with regard to the number of letters sent by him through the Dutch Diplomatic Bag, indicate that he is a person whose word is not to be trusted.

With regard to the graver suspicions we have against him we have his admission that he adopted two routes for the despatch of letters to Hungary, firstly the ordinary postal route, and secondly the Dutch Diplomatic Bag.

It is reasonable to suppose that he had some special reason for using the Bag for some letters and the ordinary post for others, and the route adopted by him in forwarding the more important letters to Hungary corresponds with that alleged to have been adopted by him in sending secret service reports out of this country.

It is also to be remembered that he volunteered the information that his brother in Vienna had had at least three interviews with Count Andrassy. Seeing that he is a struggling Jewish tailor in Pesht it is extremely improbable that he would have obtained access to a statesman in Andrassy's position unless he had information which Andrassy thought it worthwhile to receive personally.

Having regard to the whole of the circumstances of this case and, in particular, to the grave allegations made against him in the various secret service reports, it is impossible to regard de László's continued liberty in this country as other than a grave potential danger to the public safety and the defence of the realm, and his internment for the duration of the war is, accordingly, recommended.

NB Mr Basil Thomson is prepared to give evidence to the Advisory Committee on this case.

Dated: 19 Sept 1917   VG Kell
                              Competent Military Authority

5

ARREST AND HUMILIATION

O N 21 SEPTEMBER 1917, Special Branch Inspector Fred Everest, accompanied by Detective Sergeant Kirchner, took the early train to Datchet, where De László had rented a house for the summer. At 7.45 a.m. he served upon Philip Alexius László de Lombas the copy of the detention order, signed by the home secretary. De László was allowed to eat his breakfast and then the warrant was handed to him to read. He was permitted to send telegrams cancelling his engagements and then, as Everest had been instructed, he was taken to his London address (from the station at Windsor, in an attempt to stop the neighbours gossiping) where he was allowed to hand over his keys and give his wife instructions about the conduct of his affairs. He was then allowed to have lunch, had his photograph taken by the policemen and was driven to Brixton Prison and interned. The Inspector reported, 'Every courtesy compatible with duty was extended to him', which certainly appears to have been the case.

It was not necessarily so at the prison. De László was escorted by three warders who cleared out his pockets, took his razor and scissors and photographed him again, full face and profile, holding a slate with his name and number on it, in time-honoured prison style. He was horrified to discover that he was actually to be held in a cell with a heavy and locked door complete with observation window and to be counted in and out of his exercise periods. He was also horrified at the nature of the men with whom he was being held. These comprised twenty convicted foreigners:

> Four of them were German sodomites. There was another German who had been convicted of breaking into a jeweller's shop, and a Belgian who had been sentenced to twenty years penal servitude for rifling dead bodies on the battlefield. Another had kept a brothel. In fact they were mostly the lowest class imaginable, Belgians, one or two Russians, a negro, and another German who was serving a term of three years imprisonment for committing incest with his daughter, who'd had a child by him.

The press, as ever, went to town, though they had little information to go on. The *Birmingham Despatch* said the internment had caused a 'Society sensation'. The *Daily Express* commented:

> Without question, the internment of Philip De László, if only for a time, is a circumstance which will create an extraordinary amount of conversation and speculation in all of the belligerent countries. It was regarded as a 'serious' matter in well informed circles yesterday, especially having regard to the fact that he was vouched for as a would-be loyal citizen by so many influential friends in 1914.

The *Liverpool Echo* seems to have got wind of the mention of the king's opinion, as it reported that the statements sent abroad 'might have given a false impression of the views held by a personage in high authority should the letter have fallen into the hands of the Central Powers'. The *Dundee Courier* repeated the same allegation.

De László was entitled, as were all internees, to appeal against his internment, and the ever loyal Lucy organised a formidable team of lawyers and witnesses in support. The review committee met on 28 September in Westminster Hall and De László was represented by Rigby Swift KC. Lined up to give evidence on his behalf were Lord Selborne and the now Sir Arthur Lee; Lockett Agnew of the fine arts dealers Thomas Agnew and Sons; Sir Luke Fildes the painter, who gave evidence in the morning; and Lord Brabourne and Austen Chamberlain who appeared in the afternoon. The Duke of Portland and Lord Devonport sent in written evidence. The committee met in private and there is no transcript on the Home Office files, but the committee's decision was recorded and the final part is here given verbatim:

> With regard to his surreptitious communications through the diplomatic bag of a neutral country – the committee feel that they are not able to take quite the same lenient view as they have done of his conduct up till now – it is right that they should here give their impression of Mr László himself – it might almost be sufficient to say that he is an artist. He is a voluble, excitable, highly strung man, or it might even be said who will babble (the word is used advisedly) and repeat any bit of gossip he has heard. It is obvious that the position he holds as a great Society Painter enables him to pick up a good deal of this gossip. The facts he hears may be only gossip, or they may be true, but László is apparently a man of no discretion and he might quite possibly repeat anything he heard, not only to his English friends but also to his Hungarian ones without any sinister motive but merely because he is so irresponsible and has no discretion. This was an account of him which all the eminent witnesses called on his behalf appeared to agree. There was Sir Austen Chamberlain, Sir Arthur Lee, Sir Luke Fildes, Mr Howard Guinness, Lord Selborne, Lord Sheffield, Mr Lockett Agnew,

and Lord Brabourne and there were letters to a similar effect from Mr Balfour [crossed out], Lord Devonport, the Duke of Portland and Mr Baulby.

Now it is obvious –

That László has the opportunity of hearing many things;

That he has no discretion and might easily repeat what he hears without any sinister motive or any desire to injure his country or benefit the country of his birth.

The fact remains that he does hear gossip and may repeat it.

Now for some considerable time in the year 1916 he sent letters through the ordinary post to Holland – after a time he neglected the ordinary post and began to make use of the Dutch Diplomatic Bag – He says that these communications were only communications between himself and his family and also with regard to the depredation he had suffered in Hungary by reason of the hatred with which his naturalisation in this country was regarded.

He asserts that he never sent any naval, military or political news in such letters, for that we only have his own word – they were addressed to a lady who was the sister of the Foreign Minister in Holland and forwarded by her to their destination. The committee do not think it necessary to their opinion as to whether these letters contained information of the above character or not, but it is obvious there was the opportunity of sending information in that way which might be used quite indiscriminately by László, without any sinister intent, or for purposes of assisting the enemy. The committee wish distinctly to put this part of the case on the ground of opportunity – it is said by László that these communications ceased in August 1916, and that is to some extent alleged to be confirmed by the Dutch Minister, whom however the committee have not seen and the matter therefore is left as stated – László may have sent further communications or he may not.

Quite recently the French secret service received information which satisfied them that László was sending information of a political or military character from England to the Austrian Legation in Switzerland. They grounded their views upon information and documents which appeared to satisfy them. The committee have not seen the originals of these documents but only a copy of a translation of them – they are unsigned, but one of them is apparently addressed to László and says that the information which he has given to Hungary is of so valuable a character that if he desires to recover his Hungarian nationality no doubt it will be granted to him in consideration of the services he has rendered to the country of his birth. The other document purports to be a report to Hungary of the services which he has rendered, and both documents will be found attached hereto.

The committee feel –

That they have no proof of these documents

That they have no proof that they ever reached László

That even if the originals did come into existence it might have been fraudulently prepared:

By someone who desired to do László a bad turn;

By someone who desired to sow the seeds of discord between England and France, and took this very clever and adroit way of doing it.

It goes without saying that if the contents of the letter are true, László's punishment ought not to be internment but the severest penalty which the law can inflict.

The committee says that there is –

No object proof

No very strong grounds for suspicion

They however came to this conclusion, that:

Having regard to what László did in corresponding with an enemy country, and even accepting his explanation thereof

Having regard to his position, which enables him to collect information and

Having regard to his indiscretions and the way he repeats what he hears, whether innocently or with a sinister motive they could not advise the home secretary to allow him to be entirely free – they say this though they are greatly impressed by the testimony of his good faith, which all the eminent witnesses called on his behalf have spoken to.

Then comes the difficulty of knowing what to do with the safety of the realm, in the case of a man who, in view of the facts, is likely to disseminate information, not with a sinister motive, but because he is, as his own witnesses say, talkative and indiscreet.

No one of the committee thinks that it would be sufficient only to censor his correspondence – that would prevent letters reaching him but would not be a safeguard against letters going from him – is it possible then to suggest some method that would offer a middle course in this matter? It need hardly be said that no member of the committee is desirous of interning an artist of international standing for any length of time if it can be possibly avoided. The committee feel that upon the question of internment they are entitled to weigh carefully the views of Colonel Kell and Basil Thomson as to what would be an adequate safeguard which all the committee have in view, viz the safety of the realm.

Colonel Kell seems to think an internment order pure and simple would be sufficient, Mr Basil Thomson on the other hand thinks that if De László could be secluded for a time any threads of communication which he might have between Holland and this country would probably be snapped, and he would not be able to resume communication if he should desire to do so.

Now the committee feel, in this case, that the object they must try to secure is the greatest safety of the realm, coupled with the least injustice to De László, and after considerable hesitation they think that the best advice they can give to the home secretary is to intern De László to a date in December, say the 21st. It may be before the 21st December circumstances will have arisen which render the further internment of László unnecessary, but if on the 21st December László is still in internment, the committee think that his case ought to be reconsidered by then.

On 7 November 1917 De László was removed from his small cell at Brixton and taken by taxi to the Internment Camp at Holloway. The camp had formerly been a workhouse rather than a prison, so was without the high walls, bars and gates he had hated so much at Brixton. He was placed in the former infirmary building, which he shared with other naturalised British subjects, and was given a large room with four windows, which contained the furniture of the former resident Baron von Bissing (brother of the former German governor of Belgium, interned in 1915 and recently released to house arrest on grounds of ill-health), who had arranged with Lucy De László to leave it (and Von Bissing's personal servant) for him. Among his companions were Dr Whitehead, an Austrian-born chemist naturalised in South Africa, and Herr Ahlers, former German consul-general, both interned after the sinking of the *Lusitania*. It was an altogether more congenial arrangement than at Brixton, and De László was given a place at the 'aristocrat table'. Here, he described:

> We were served by a waiter from the German camp and our cook had been a chef at the Hotel Cecil. I felt happy to be among intelligent men, to have a comfortable room and to be able to go out into the garden when I liked … I thanked God that I was able to sleep in a decent bed again, and was free of the cell door with the observation glass in it which had upset my nerves so much at Brixton.

6

NAMES, ADDRESSES AND THE ELUSIVE MADAME G

D E LÁSZLÓ WAS certain to launch a further appeal against his internment to Lord Sankey and the internment review committee. To preserve the secrecy of MI5's involvement as far as possible, Thomson took over the case and contacted Bigham in Paris directly asking for information.

Bigham's reply set out carefully the conditions on which the French were prepared to assist. Their conditions, quite natural given the highly secret nature of their source, were to hamstring any future attempts to prosecute De László for espionage. Having sent translations of three letters he went on to explain:

> These were got at the house of the Austrian Military Attaché at Berne, but neither this, nor the fact that we have received them from the French must be alluded to in any way whatsoever ... I have had them retranslated into English so that if it is necessary to suggest they were procured from an agent it may be presumed it was from one of our own people. This is what the French desire and I have promised that we would not do anything that might disclose the means they had of getting the information.

At some date (probably the end of September 1917 as it was forwarded to the Home Office on 29 September), MI5 received a
copy of another letter to De László from Geneva, from the same
source that had produced the letter dated 14 June (which tends to
preclude Maundy Gregory as the agent who obtained it). It read:

> My dear friend
>   Don't bear me malice if I charge you with a new mission.
> I will not charge you with explications, reasons etc. Those are
> things only necessary with people whose zeal needs warming up
> and we are not like that. I ask you to collaborate with us in our
> pacifist propaganda. As soon as I receive your reply I will let you
> have details.
>   I am very anxious about Madame G. Be on your guard. Have
> I told you already that my brother in law died suddenly some
> weeks ago. He left a very large fortune.

Though too late to be used before the committee, this seemed
to confirm the connection with the mysterious Madame G and
the involvement of De László with pacifist propaganda.

There was a growing necessity, for Austria at least, to pull
out of the war. By early 1917 Austria-Hungary was in deep
trouble and in desperate need of peace. The old emperor,
Franz Josef, whom De László had so esteemed, had died in
November 1916 and been succeeded by Karl, nephew of
Archduke Franz Ferdinand whose assassination had precipi-
tated the war. Karl was painfully aware that the country was
on the verge of collapse. It had gone to war optimistic of a
rapid victory over both Serbia and Russia and had suffered
severe casualties on both fronts. By early 1917 there were
nearly two million Austro-Hungarian prisoners in Russia
alone. Italy's surprise (and to the Austrians, treacherous) entry
into the war on the side of the Allies in May 1915 created a

third front. Even though the Italians behaved in exactly the way caricatured in *Blackadder Goes Forth* and *Oh! What a Lovely War*, hurling poorly armed and trained troops against a series of well-defended positions, they still inflicted a growing number of casualties as they inched forward and gradually learned the lessons of modern warfare.

Over the winter of 1915, Austria had already called up men aged between 49 and 53; there had been food riots during 1915 too and the harsh winter of 1916–17 made things far worse. Industrial output was in steep decline and coal production was falling rapidly because so many miners had been called up. The British knew this perfectly well because a Foreign Office official, W.G. Max Müller, was producing a series of analyses of Austria's economic performance. The ever-vigilant censorship service had also been picking up information about conditions within Austria-Hungary throughout the war. From mail carried on neutral steamers (which were diverted into British ports throughout the world and the mail they carried opened) came stories of rationing, failing food supplies and near-starvation. A letter from Moravia to the United States, written in August 1916, complained:

> Oh! It really is enough to drive one mad. The people tear the potatoes out of the earth when they should still be flowering to have something for their hunger. Really you cannot believe the awful hunger … If we starve you cannot help us: and that is bound to happen if the war does not come to an end soon.

A letter from Budapest to the USA in October 1916 read, 'Many things are 5 and 10 times as expensive in peace time. From last week we have two meat and fishless days and 1 greenless day. Silver is fast disappearing, a few days ago all the nickel and copper coins had disappeared.' Another writer wrote,

'We have quite enough poverty here, they are taking away the corn, removing the bells from the churches, sealing up the grain and do not allow it to be ground.' A letter from Hungary to the United States in November advised that all corn and maize had to be delivered to the military authorities, that they had not had sugar or oil for three months and that no meat could be purchased. It was clear that government rationing schemes weren't working; a relatively wealthy peasant wrote that the government had taken over the provision of food, but even they couldn't provide something that didn't exist. Another writer told his American relatives that everyone had had to give up their copper and brass utensils and the churches had had to donate one or two of their bells. The censors noted that their Austrian equivalents had previously carefully deleted any references to these kind of matters (not realising the British censors could 'restore' the deletion), but now they seemed to be letting them through.

It was becoming clear that it was only a matter of time before the empire collapsed. The emperor Karl had been warned by his foreign minister, Count Czernin, that the exhausted state of the army and food shortages might result in revolution and rebellion among the many nationalities that made up the empire. With the Allies beginning to discuss future peace terms, giving liberty to those very minorities, Karl approached them with terms of his own in March 1917. These included German withdrawal from Belgium and France (including Alsace-Lorraine), and Serbian independence. There were no proposals dealing with Italy so the Allies rejected them. Conditions in Austria were continuing to deteriorate, however, and peace was becoming increasingly necessary. It was in this environment that allegations of De László spreading pro-Austrian peace propaganda among his upper-class clients caused such concern.

The Elusive Madame G

Though De László's hearing was told that it had not been possible to locate the elusive Madame G, there is one indication that perhaps MI5 managed to do so, but were unable to make the case for an arrest. There are two index cards for Foreign Office correspondence for 1918 at TNA naming Leopold Samuel Gompertz and Henrietta Charlotte Gompertz. They were allowed to leave Britain, but only with a visa that specified they were not allowed to return. The file that the papers are related to still exists (unfortunately without most of its contents), and the covering memorandum was issued by MI5.E.2. which had clearly circulated the latest list of non-return visas to military control offices around the world.

The Madame G in question had been born on 3 February 1864 in Frankfurt Main as Henrietta Charlotte Wetzlar, daughter of a prominent Austrian banker. She had married Leopold Gompertz, of the Gompertz banking family, in Amsterdam in 1885. Leopold presumably represented the Wertheim and Gompertz Bank in London.

In April 1915, MI5 had been warned by Consul Maxse in Rotterdam that the Germans were buying the services of Dutch agents who were to live in London and report from there. Dutch researcher Edwin Ruis, an expert on the intelligence activities of both sides in Holland, advises:

> Many Dutch Jews were originally from Germany or the Habsburg empire and sympathetic to Germany. German intelligence officers did recruit German wives of Dutch citizens to spy. A famous case is Dr Willy Brandt who did not only recruit the known spy Lizzy Wertheim, but who also tried to recruit other German women in the Netherlands.

Brandt, whose doctorate was in economics, had recruited agents for the army intelligence *Sektion* IIIb, and from December 1914 worked for German naval intelligence. MI5 was certainly aware of Dr Brandt's existence as his name and address had been signalled (presumably by Tinsley of SIS or Consul Maxse) to them on 6 February 1915 as being a post box used by the German secret service, and his address was put on the censorship watch list. Brandt is also named in MI5's historical report on convicted spy Lizzie Wertheim as being her German contact in Holland (National Archives reference KV 1/42).

The firm of Wertheim and Gompertz was under suspicion in its own right. In July 1915 the *AlgemeenHandelsblad* newspaper had reported that the bank had received 100 cases of gold to the value of 5 million kronen from the Austrian government. In October 1915 it was suspected of being involved in the shipment of gold from Germans in the USA to Holland for the credit of German banks.

On 6 December 1915 the chief censor advised the Foreign Office:

> Wertheim and Gompertz of 30 Amstelstraat, Amsterdam, are the Firm with whom Sutro Brothers and Company, of New York, suggested the arrangement of a cable code to deceive the Censor into thinking that sales of securities on account of Amsterdam (and therefore possibly Germany) to New York were really sales by New York to Amsterdam. Sutro Bros and Company, of 44 Pine Street, New York, have a branch office in Berlin under Meyerhof who is presumably the man mentioned in Sir C Spring's telegram. Wertheim and Gompertz are apparently the channel for messages, gold and securities between Meyerhof of Berlin and Sutro Brothers of New York (or the National City Bank of New York).

The British Admiralty intercepted a telegram, dated 1 November 1915, from National City Bank, New York, to Ernst Meyerhof & Co., Berlin, reading, 'Inform Wertheim and Gompertz that we will ship the gold to the extent of their credit balance under their risk our responsibility to end with delivery of gold to steamship.'

Wertheim and Gompertz were closely aligned with the American bank Kuhn Loeb, and Sir Ernest Cassel, in railways and similar dealings. Sutro Bros was a New York investment bank that was basically a subsidiary of Kuhn Loeb. The British were well aware that a link to Kuhn Loeb meant one to Paul Warburg, the naturalised American banker of German origin, to one degree or another, and that meant a link to Germany, where Warburg remained a partner in his family-owned bank.

Sutro Bros had been founded by Lionel and Richard Sutro, American-born brothers of German-Jewish ancestry. The leading figure during the war was Richard, amongst whose friends was Kuhn Loeb's Otto Kahn. American Bureau of Investigation (the predecessor of the FBI) files contain nothing on Richard Sutro or Sutro Bros per se, but they do note that Theodore Sutro, a New York attorney, possibly a German-born cousin, was very active in the German National Alliance and later the Friends of Peace, which brought him under suspicion. There is also mention of a Victor Sutro, a broker with Sutro and Kimbley, who shows up as a suspected pro-German.

Because of these suspicions, Wertheim and Gompertz were placed on the British government's trade black list and a number of their securities in London were seized. It was only in mid-1916, after they joined the Netherlands Overseas Trust, an organisation founded in November 1914 to control Dutch trade and guarantee that imports were not re-exported to Germany, that they were gradually removed from the black list and able to resume dealings abroad.

While investigations into Madame G were carried out, MI5 took De László's address book and ran his contacts through its, by now extensive, index of suspects. Every report submitted to MI5 by its own small number of agents, by the police, SIS agents abroad, the censorship department and naval intelligence's worldwide network of naval consuls, as well as from the public and press, were examined by officers and marked for indexing in a huge card index. Cards were generally held under the name of a person but suspect addresses were also 'carded' and there were various subject headings, all of which had to be cross-referenced. The whole business of carding, cross-referencing and filing was carried out by teams of mainly women clerks recruited from businesses, the best schools, and women's colleges at university. Like the officers, many of them spoke several languages and some had travelled extensively. It was hard work. Sir Everard Radcliffe recorded in his unpublished memoir, 'We were kept very hard at work at MI5, having one Sunday in two free, and a very occasional half day, and having to do one all-night duty once a fortnight.'

As well as the initial carding and cross-referencing, the women staff also did the 'look ups', finding references to suspects from previous reports. This required a lot of ingenuity, and knowledge of foreign languages was invaluable in trying to tease out possible misspellings of foreign names or addresses. They would draw up a list of definite, likely and possible matches and submit them to the officer who would then examine the suggested reports in detail and decide which were relevant. When sufficient information was gathered to convince them that the suspect required it, the reports were copied and filed together in a Personal File (PF). These were initially held alphabetically but the system was changed to a strictly numerical sequence when it was realised it made filing easier; new files could be added to the end of the run rather than having to slot them into place. Other information, once analysed, was used to draw up black lists of suspect companies and addresses to be used by port security officers examining travellers entering the country and for consuls and passport control officers abroad who issued (or didn't issue) visas for foreigners to visit the UK or the empire.

Given the close involvement of Holland and Dutch subjects in the case it was inevitable that MI5 turned to its man in Rotterdam Richard Tinsley, a former merchant navy officer and member of the Royal Naval Reserve, and now a serving SIS officer of great experience. Before the war he had been employed by the Uranium Shipping Co., which took Russian emigrants to the USA. He had been expelled briefly from Holland for breaking Dutch law by landing emigrants without permission, but was back in business at the start of the war and helped Consul Maxse deal with refugees from Belgium while at the same time helping him set up a rudimentary intelligence gathering system. When Maxse was warned off intelligence work by the Foreign Office because of his diplomatic position (though, as we shall see, this was ignored), Tinsley took over the intelligence side and was transferred to SIS and promoted to the rank of commander in the RNR.

From his Uranium Shipping Office he ran extensive networks of agents in occupied Belgium and France reporting on military information, particularly train movements. He also reported on Dutch trade with Germany (vital in enforcing the economic blockade), probably by bribing or suborning Dutch customs officials, and supplied pacifist propaganda to German socialists to help them encourage desertion into neutral Holland by German troops (from whom he gathered intelligence). He also ran probably the best British spy of the war, a renegade German codenamed H16 or R16, who was a naval engineer who could travel extensively in the naval dockyards. His real name was Otto Kruger and he supplied first-class information on the state of the German fleet and naval developments, never more so than shortly after Jutland when he sent in a detailed report on the extensive damage suffered.

From MI5's perspective it was Tinsley's close watch on the activities of the German Secret Service that mattered most. Their secret addresses were watched, as were their contacts. It seems likely he ran the double agent codenamed COMO, an American who, as a neutral, was able to visit Britain and who reported on his fellow German agents through Tinsley to MI5. It was through Tinsley (codenamed T) that details of prospective agents were received, and he was instrumental in the capture of several spies and in providing information that allowed MI5's port security prevent them landing in Britain.

Whereas all reports received by MI5 from other sources passed through the registry system before being forwarded to the relevant section, Tinsley's reports were considered so valuable and important that they were sent straight to the investigators of G Division unopened. Sir Everard Radcliffe, a former captain of Yorkshire County Cricket Club who served with MI5 from 1916 to 1919, left an unpublished memoir of his service which is held by the Liddle Archive at Leeds University, and it confirms the respect in which Tinsley was held, at least within MI5: 'Many were the interesting cases, but what remains most vividly in my mind was the brilliance of our Agent in Holland, who rarely failed to advise when an important spy was en route to England, and almost invariably was able to apprise for what purpose and where he intended to go.'

De László's address book produced a total of twenty-nine persons who had come to MI5's attention in one way or another. In some ways they are a raggle-taggle bunch and one or two seem, frankly, facile, and were even commented upon as such by an unknown hand. Some were Austrian or Hungarian, as one might suspect, such as von Offenheim, an Austrian subject and formerly a rich merchant in London. He was described as having 'left with Austrian Ambassador at beginning of the war, withdrawing a large sum of money in notes and gold'. Mrs Knatchbull Huggesson of 43 Norfolk Square (by 1917 now Lady Braeburn) and her sister Mrs Oswald Crawford were noted as being 'Daughters of Hermann von Flisch Brommingen, Imperial Councillor of Vienna. Many allegations respecting them, but nothing suspicious proved.' There was an address for Countess Hoyos, sister of the Austrian chargé d'affaires at Christiania (now Oslo, in Norway), who was acting for Germany there, but there were no specific allegations.

Mrs Wood of 23 Rutland Court, Kensington, was the Hungarian-born Countess Rosa Lonyay before she married George Jarvis Wood, an Englishman and at one time an unpaid attaché in Vienna. During the war he had enlisted in the Intelligence Corps and later became a captain and king's messenger. Mrs Wood had come to MI5's attention when, early in the war, she managed to get two German servants exempted from repatriation on her own bond of £50. The servants had eventually been repatriated anyway, on 29 July 1916.

De László readily admitted knowing Eugene De Weress, a Hungarian student who was studying in Britain on the outbreak of war but who was now interned. The main point about MI5 mentioning him seemed to be his connection with the 'notorious' Frederick Lawrence Rawson, formerly a director of various companies including the British Union and National Insurance Co., who had drifted into Theosophism and begun to prophesy about the course of the war and to offer hope that 'scientific' prayer would both shorten the war and give long-distance comfort to the wounded. His meetings were well attended but also attracted the attentions of the *Daily Mail* which ran a series of debunking articles about him and his claimed occult powers. These provoked opposition to his meetings and the attentions of the police. On 16 January 1917, the police raided his business property in

Regent Street (where he described himself as a 'Divine Healer'), where there was a large number of clerks and typists and which received and sent large volumes of mail. Large amounts of correspondence and paperwork were taken away. Two days previously, the police had gone to the address and detained a Hungarian employee (presumably De Weress) who had been sent to an internment camp. They raided Rawson's rooms, where they also took away books and papers to Scotland Yard. No charges appear to have been brought against Rawson who continued his work, though on a much reduced scale.

Dezol, or Desiderius, Polanyi was described as 'Hungarian, alien enemy' with a son who had returned to Hungary on the outbreak of war and who was now serving in the Hungarian army, and a daughter who was a Red Cross nurse engaged with the same forces. Polanyi was noted as having casual employment in London with German alien Thospam, a dealer in cameras, whose factory was in Hamburg.

Polanyi had first come to Britain in May 1914 from his native Hungary in connection with a patent for motion pictures. Despite his children's military connections the only bad mark against Polanyi himself was a comment from a businessman with whom he had had dealings that he did not know the difference between good and evil. There was also the curious matter that Polanyi had, at one point, given his address as St Joseph's Convent, Hendon, a religious foundation which seemed to consist of forty or so nuns, many of whom were of German origin. When he was traced by MI5 he gave the reason that he was temporarily without a permanent address and had arranged for a friend in the convent to receive mail on his behalf. Polanyi had not been repatriated to Hungary, even though he was over the age of 55, because he was found to be doing important chemical work for a British company and it was decided it was better his knowledge was retained in Britain than given to the enemy.

It was only natural that De László should have known Paul G. Konody of the Albany, Piccadilly, a naturalised British former Austro-Hungarian art critic. Like so many foreigners or naturalised subjects he was reported to have strong anti-British sympathies, but no reliable evidence had yet been obtained.

Similar unsubstantiated allegations had been made against Alexander Gross, a former Hungarian naturalised as British, the managing director of Geographia Ltd of 55 Fleet Street, private address 'Buda Pesth', Hampstead, who made aviation and other maps. Gross had first come to MI5's attention in March 1912 when his company had applied to various railway companies for plans of their systems. The business was investigated but nothing detrimental was found. On 5 August 1914 the company's premises had been searched by the police, but again, nothing had been found. Though MI5's file contained some anonymous allegations against him, and it had a record of a telephone conversation (presumably overheard by an operator) between Gross and his office about a map of a recent naval battle, the only matter of substance related to his employment of some men of 'bad character and shady methods' among his sales force.

Given the allegations that De László was involved in Austrian peace propaganda, MI5 must have been interested in any connections he had with J Szebenyei of Normanhurst, 11 Park Avenue, Golders Green. As Hungarian correspondent of the *Morning Post*, Szebenyei was accused, in January 1917, of using forged letters, purporting to come from Hungary, as the basis for pro-peace articles in the newspaper. Though his editor stood by him, investigations suggested that he was, at the very least, an unwitting participant in an enemy plot to spread propaganda in Britain and he was interned. It seems possible that Szebenyei was the man who provoked the troubles in Hungary by revealing De László's naturalisation.

There were several individuals alleged to have had contact at some time with the enemy secret services. One such was Professor Antonio Cippico, who was Professor of Italian at the University of London. Unfortunately for him, though an out-and-out Italian nationalist, he had been born in Trieste which made him legally an Austrian citizen and therefore subject to suspicion. Travelling to London with the approval of the Italian Government (then neutral), he had tried to get permission to raise a foreign legion in Britain but this had been refused. He had made frequent patriotic speeches on behalf of the Italian Government, who solved his problems with the British authorities for him by naturalising him by royal decree in April 1915 (which was actually in contravention of an Italian law forbidding naturalisation of Austrians in time of crisis). Cippico had been reported by Chevalier Ricci, the honorary secretary of the Dante Society, to be a native of Austria, an agent of von Buelow's and a spy. The Italian Consulate, however, regarded Cippico as a loyal Italian and Ricci as a blackguard.

An otherwise unidentified Mrs Leeds was reported as a visitor to Count Talleyrand de Perigord who was himself reported as being of the German Intelligence Service, but there were no further details.

The Comte de Soissons was an art critic and, at the very least, an acquaintance of De László, but he was also a friend of Baroness Nerembourger (aka Mrs Meyer), described by MI5 as 'the lady in the Malcolm case who was said to be a spy'. Lieutenant Douglas Malcolm was an army officer accused of murdering a foreigner who went under the name Count de Borch (real name Anton Baumberg) who, Malcolm claimed, was trying to seduce his wife. Malcolm shot him dead and was tried for murder in September 1917. Interestingly, at the initial inquest, evidence was given that Baumberg had been questioned at Scotland Yard by Mr Curtis Bennett and Major Charles Dunlop (both MI5 officers, though this is not referred to) about his identity and about a woman known as 'The Countess', aka Mrs Meyer, with whom he had lived and who was believed to be a spy. Also of interest is the fact that Malcolm had recently been to Scotland Yard and had an interview with the assistant commissioner (Basil Thomson) to discuss Baumberg and seems to have come away with the impression that he was both a white slaver and an enemy agent. Much of this came out at the subsequent murder trial and, as a result, Malcolm was acquitted after the jury took just twenty minutes to deliberate.

Given De László's Dutch connections it's hardly surprising that some Dutchmen featured in the list. Graf Schimmelpenninck de Nyenhus, a Dutch nobleman with a German wife, was noted as 'Appears in the list of pro-German nobles compiled by our representative', the representative presumably being the ubiquitous Richard Tinsley. Count William Bentinck of Harley Street and former attaché at the German Embassy in London had been allowed to leave London in 1914 because of both his diplomatic status and his insistence he was actually Dutch. Reports had reached MI5 that he had subsequently fought for Germany in the Prussian Garde du Corps. By 1917 he was again claiming to be neutral, and living in Holland, where he was reported to be in a continual relationship with German legation. Tellingly, given De László's history, letters from England were believed to go to him by the Dutch official bag.

Wilhelm von Mallinckrodt of Hausahms, 2 Rue Gounod, Antwerp, was believed to be the same Mallinckrodt of W Mallinckrodt & Co., Antwerp, who had been expelled from Belgium at the commencement of the war as a German agent, but had subsequently returned and sent supplies to the German army. Described as a very wealthy man, he was now reported to be chief of the *Kommandantur* in Liege, and Mallinckrodt & Co.'s premises were reported to be the rendezvous of German agents. Consul Maxse, who, despite having been warned off by the Foreign

Office, ran a parallel, even more secret network of British agents in Holland to Richard Tinsley, reported Mallinckrodt as a German agent in November 1915. Maxse also advised the Foreign Office that one of his companies had set up an office in Rotterdam under a false name in order to disguise his connection to it.

Perhaps most interesting and worrying, De László had the address of one Jonkheer E.J.C. Greven, a lieutenant in the Dutch army. Greven had come to England three times previously during the war. He had visited Aldershot, home of the British army, and was there shown a great deal on the recommendation of the British military attaché. A British army officer who had met him at the Regent Palace Hotel in London had reported him as a probable spy because he asked so many questions about military matters. He had also excited similar suspicions at Avonmouth on a visit there. Consul Maxse had reported, in February 1917, that Greven was believed to be in German pay and to have worked for Germany in England in 1915.

There was one German connection that also linked closely to Holland. Baroness von Diergardt was described as 'Hostess of Graham [sic] Scott, who was detained under (DORA) Regulation 14B', presumably during the visit to Holland that led to his detention. The possible connection with Scott would have fascinated MI5. The 34-year-old Graeme Scott had initially come under suspicion while working as a journalist in The Hague – he appeared to be too friendly with the German military attaché, who ran the local intelligence organisation. On his return to England, MI5 invoked DRR 14, and ordered him to live on the Isle of Man. In July 1915 it then interned him under DRR 14B on the grounds that it seemed neither 'safe to leave him at large or permit him to go abroad'. Scott was sent to the 'Islington Camp' – the old Islington workhouse used for internment – and put in the '14B Block' with Ferdinand Kehrhahn, a socialist activist. In November 1916

Scott, Kehrhahn, and another 14B internee named Hodgson escaped by cutting the wire over a window, and went on the run. There was a huge police operation to find them. Scott and Hodgson were soon recaptured, but Kehrhahn got all the way to New York before being detained and sent back.

There were a few Americans who had come under suspicion. Mrs Wm Payne Thompson of 703 Thames St, Newport, USA, was reported, presumably by the Censorship Department, to be in constant communication with Germany. An unnamed captain of an unnamed German submarine was said to have called on her when he landed in America (on an unspecified date). Countess Helena Pourtales of 14 Portman Square, London, was described as an American, married to a Swiss who had served in the German army. She had German relations, including a son-in-law now in the German army and a cousin who had been German ambassador at Petrograd at the outbreak of the war. She had been to Germany with her daughters. She also received, in England, German newspapers printed in English for American use. In addition, she was related to a Countess R. de Pourtales, residing in Germany, who had been to America to visit her relative Count Bernsdorf, the German ambassador to the USA.

At the end of 1916, MI5, with the assistance of SIS agents in New York, had broken up a spy ring involving American journalists recruited in the USA by German intelligence, who had then gone to Holland from where they could travel to Britain and gather information before returning to Holland to report it. They noted that De László held an address for one Walter Roberts, who was connected with the *New York Herald* and, in particular, with one Bennett, described as a pro-German American journalist. Finally, among the Americans, though in what connection De László was supposed to know him (except perhaps as a target for one of his scams) there was Henry Beigel, who had been deported to America as an undesirable alien. Born in Germany, Beigel was a naturalised American citizen and described as a 'Notorious swindler, cardsharper and procurer'.

Then, of course, there were the Germans. One can quite understand why De László would have known George Lauter, a German portrait painter who was resident in London pre-war. Lauter was interned and afterwards repatriated. Given also De László's connection to the kaiser's court it is perhaps easy to understand why he had addresses for Count Eulenberg, 'The notorious bosom friend of the kaiser' as well as Prince Hans Heinrich of Pless, Count Fritz Hochberg and Countess Hoyos, all described as German and all related, and Prince Salm-Salm of Arnholt, Westphalia, Germany, a Prussian cavalry officer married to the daughter of Archduke Frederick, in command of Austrian armies. Both the prince and his wife were interned at Gibraltar at the outbreak of war, but were later exchanged for an English prisoner of war. The prince had been killed later in the war, but the princess was, at present, in Switzerland making violent propaganda in favour of the Central Empires. Connected to her was the widow of the late Max Grunelius, a German banker at Frankfurt and formerly a 'Smart friend of the Emperor' who was described as being a friend of Princess Salm-Salm, living in Switzerland and suspected of giving information to Germany.

There were others, though none perhaps so exalted. R. von Hochenhecher was described as 'Late German officer now in Holland'. H. Loeffler was the son of a naturalised British subject of German origin, married to a Swede, the daughter of General Balck, 'who is thoroughly pro-German, and a friend of German Minister at Stockholm. His wife is great friend of the German Minister's daughter.' Theodore von Guillaume, another contact, was a German subject of 45 Deutscher Ring, Cologne, and head of the firm of Felten and Guillaume, submarine cable manufacturers. He had been reported as seen in London on 20 June 1917, but had not been traced.

There were a couple of Germans said to have connections with the enemy secret services. One was Rudolph Said-Ruete, formerly of 39 Bramham Gardens, a German subject now in Switzerland, married to one of the Monds and formerly manager of the Cairo branch of Deutsche Orient Bank. Said-Ruete wrote articles entitled 'England's War Guiltiness' and 'Interviewed at Potsdam' etc. He was a promoter of the British Progressive Club, Zurich, the leader of which was Mostevitch, a 'notorious Hungarian spy'. Then there was Hans R. Schulze of Berlin. In addition to appearing in De László's address book, his name was also found in the papers of one Holzamner, a 'known Austrian spy'.

One curious inclusion was the Asiatic Trading Co. chairman, H.N. Anderson, a Dane described as 'a man of low origin who has made his money in doubtful ways'. A friend of the Kaiser, Anderson had visited him in Berlin in the summer of 1916. As a neutral, Anderson travelled to and from Petrograd, Berlin, Copenhagen and London, which presumably gave him ample opportunities for both spying and carrying secret messages. His company now ran the German Kosmos shipping line along routes on the west coast of South and Central America. Anderson was a friend of Queen Alexandra's; her brother Prince Waldemar was said to be a shareholder in East Asiatic Co. Other shareholders were George of Greece, the King of Siam, the Czar and the Kaiser, also the Danske Bank, the Danish branch of Deutsche Bank. MI5 noted, 'It is believed that not a single ship of EAST ASIATIC CO has been sunk during the war.' Someone added a pencil note later, 'Not likely on the West Coast of America' which is, of course, correct, but given Anderson's movements it would seem likely the company ran other routes.'

There were a few others. Baron Francis Elanger was a naturalised British subject of German origin, now living in Tunis and suspected of being in enemy pay. Francis Trippel, alias Franz Heinrich Trippel of St James Street, Piccadilly, was an ex-soldier in the German army. He had been a crammer and schoolmaster between 1895 and 1910, then secretary to Sir Max Waechter, German entrepreneur, art collector and philanthropist. Trippel travelled with him abroad and met the Kaiser in 1910. Still based in London, Trippel was obviously being watched as MI5 knew he was suddenly in possession of large sums of money and had given £1,000 to the Union Jack Club. He apparently made money by commission on subscriptions from the public for war charities. MI5 considered him a 'Very suspicious character, unscrupulous and connected with the Peace League'.

Baron Schroeder, a German, had, like De László, naturalised after the start of the war, but had a son in the German army. He was known to have subscribed to the Kaiser's Jubilee Fund and been present at the celebratory dinner. He had, said MI5, provided money to pay off the mortgage on the German Club after the start of the war. There is a further note, 'According to young [sic] De László is keeping champagne to drink to "Der Tag".' A pencilled remark next to this entry reads, 'This is a ridiculous note.'

Linked to Baron Schroeder was Frank Tiarks, his business partner. MI5 said he was married to a German woman who had two sons fighting for Germany. He had also been reported to have German sympathies. The reference is peculiar, especially as Tiarks was, at the time MI5 wrote about him, a lieutenant commander in the Royal Naval Volunteer Reserve and engaged in particularly secret work for Naval Intelligence, working in Admiralty Room 40 where the naval code breakers were busily engaged in breaking German ciphers. There's also absolutely no truth in the story that his German-born wife, whom he had married in 1900 when she was just 24, had two sons serving in the German army. It looks horribly as if MI5 had just jotted down some rumours about him and not bothered to investigate them before passing them on.

Given De László's supposed peace propaganda activities, why was he holding an address for Robert Dell, a keen pacifist and Fabian Society member, living in Paris and acting as correspondent for the *Manchester Guardian*? As early as 1915, Dell had written that France had lost all her men and could not go on, and should make a separate peace if England insisted on fighting further. He later wrote a book on peace. He was described by MI5 as blaming England and France for the war as much as Germany.

Only one person on the list had the dubious honour of already having a file prepared on them. This was Lady Suffolk (file reference V.F. 370/15), née Leiter, who, MI5 noted, 'After outbreak of war went from Paris to Baden-Baden. Reported to have received a visit and a bouquet of flowers from Kaiser's second son, who provided passports out of Germany for her and her maid.'

It's a hard list to analyse given there's nothing to say how many people were in the address book in total and some of the entries (that of Frank Tiarks, for example) are quite simply wrong. Many of the people were the kind of 'high society' contacts that an internationally famous portrait painter might be expected to know – and whose cosmopolitan (we might these days call it celebrity) lifestyle meant that they in turn were in close contact with, related to, or married into foreign families. Lady Suffolk is one of these, as were Countess Portales and the various German aristocrats. De László's former Hungarian nationality and known support for charities that helped poorer members of the community in Britain would surely explain his contacts with many of his former countrymen.

One or two alleged contacts with people suspected (at least) of being enemy agents are harder to explain. Why an address for Jonkheer Greven, for example? Jonkheer is a very minor Dutch noble rank, hardly on a par with the German, Austrian and British nobility De László knew. He was only a lieutenant so he was probably quite young. That the Dutch themselves might send a young officer to Britain, officially or unofficially, to gather information is hardly surprising – but Maxse's intelligence organisation, which reached into the heart of the Dutch government and made use of contacts he had built up over years as British consul, tended to produce accurate information, based as it frequently was on Dutch police and military sources. Greven was, almost certainly, some kind of German spy. Wilhelm von Mallinckrodt, provided the identification is correct, is also hard to understand, not being of the normal class of De László's contacts and, again, having been identified by Maxse's agency, likely to have been a German agent.

Most telling, perhaps, are the number of contacts who were known, or said to be, involved in peace propaganda on behalf of the Central Powers or in advocating anti-war sentiment. There was Robert Dell, with his own Dutch connections through his work for *Der Telegraaf*; Rudolph Said-Ruete, with his own articles condemning England's part in the war; Princess Salm-Salm, in Switzerland making her violent propaganda in favour of the Central Empires; and Countess Helena Pourtales, with her English-language German newspapers for America.

7

INTERNMENT AND
CONTROVERSY

MI5'S REPORT ON the address book was submitted to the Home Office on 18 December, just in time to be presented to the forthcoming review of De László's case. Though nothing conclusive could be proven from De László's contacts in his address book, the presence of certain names, linked to either espionage or enemy peace propaganda, were bound to strengthen MI5's concerns that here was a man who was a risk to the security of the realm.

As well as their analysis of his address book, MI5 presented a letter from Colonel Kell setting out his objections to an immediate release:

Short of the war being over by the 21st December and unless any new factors arise which will conclusively prove that an injustice has been committed in interning László or that his health is in grave peril, I cannot foresee any circumstances which are likely to call for any alteration in the committee's decision of internment.

I cannot agree that in so short a time the threads of which he might have between Holland and this country would probably be snapped and that he would not be able to resume communications, if he should desire to do so.

His channel of communication still remains and his friends in Holland will doubtless still exist, who can transmit whatever he chooses to send them, either by bag or by hand.

I admit the case has been one of considerable difficulty and I have, I think, been privileged to have been consulted in this case by the committee more than in any other. I have therefore had the opportunity of realizing some if not all of the difficulties with which the Committee have been confronted and their endeavours to arrive at a just and fair solution of the case.

M.I.5.   Signed by Vernon Kell

Once again there is no transcript of the actual hearing, but the committee conclusion exists and is given here in its entirety:

The committee sat to reconsider the case of Mr De László. They heard Mr De László himself and several other witnesses who he desired to call.

Since the last occasion a list had been prepared for the committee of the names and addresses of certain people appearing in Mr László's address books. The committee were informed that many of these people are strongly pro-German in sympathy and some of them were said to be in touch with German spies. The committee were not able to say whether this is so or not, but they put some of the names to Mr László, whose reply was that they were persons who had come to him either to be painted, or upon subjects connected to art, or art criticism.

In addition to this there was a letter from Geneva purporting to be written on 16th July last (gives detail of letter) … The letter is unsigned, but purports to be addressed to a member of the German Legation at Berlin. Beyond that the committee know nothing about it, but it appears to be of a similar character to those scheduled to the committee's last report to which they beg to refer.

A great grievance was made by all the witnesses that it was generally thought that some sinister interpretation could be attached to the fact that Mr László applied for naturalisation after the war.

The committee dealt specifically with this matter on page 3 of their previous report and they sum it up by saying 'no sinister conclusion can be drawn from the circumstances surrounding his naturalisation'.

In the event of future questions being asked in the House of Commons on this point the authorities might consider whether it would not be an act of justice both to Mr László and to sponsors, that this point should be made clear.

Coming to the main point of the case, the committee do not see their way to alter the advice which they gave to the home secretary in their first report, and they are of the opinion that Mr De László's internment should be continued.

John Hankey, on behalf of the advisory committee
20th December 1917

De László's friends campaigned to have him released, to no avail. Jerome K. Jerome, author of *Three Men in a Boat*, launched a campaign among his fellow artists but was surprised by the poor response. In part this was because of a continuing campaign by the press against De László, but also because, De László later claimed, his fellow portrait painter Sir Arthur Stockdale Cope RA organised a surreptitious campaign of his own against him, assisted by his friend Admiral Sir Reginald Hall, Director of Naval Intelligence. Hall was without doubt the most important man in the British intelligence community, with huge resources, huge influence and a finger in every intelligence pie. He would have known the full details of MI5's case if any man outside the organisation did. It's interesting that he might have had some influence, behind the scenes, in keeping De László interned. The internment was now set, unless there was an unexpected development, to last until the end of the war.

Despite the more relaxed conditions in the Holloway Internment Camp, the stress of De László's situation continued to bear down on him. Many of his friends seemed to have abandoned him, virtually all the clubs he had been a member of removed his name from their lists, Eton College refused to accept his sons though they had been on its books for many years, and, with no new income coming in, many sitters who owed him money were reluctant to pay up. He was paying for his own food as he had done throughout his internment and he had many other financial commitments. Though it is claimed that he had a nervous breakdown as a result of his worries, this isn't borne out by the Home Office files, but a succession of medical reports commissioned by Lucy, even if written by sympathetic doctors, show a steady decline in his condition.

On 5 March 1918, Dr E.F. Eyre, the Islington camp doctor reported:

P de László's condition is becoming serious, he is suffering from intense headache of a constricting type and neuritis of right side, also intestinal muscular ateny, which causes constipation. Mentally his depression is very great. The most serious point about his condition is the weakening of his Cardio-Vascular System, his pulse having been irregular (Arrhythmia) but is now changed to a very weak and slow action (Brachychardia).

His condition at present is one that if not very early relieved will develop into Arterio-Schlerosis. This condition has the effect of reducing even a man of abilities to mediocrity.

The one and only treatment for the case is release from internment as soon as possible.

A doctor appointed by the Home Office visited the camp and reported:

> On the 26th February 1918 I examined Mr P A Lazlo de Lombas … He presents a healthy appearance, has a good colour, and his circulation to all outward appearance is normal. He says he suffers much from constipation but he looks well nourished, his tongue is clean, and there is no apparent accumulation of faeces in the lower bowel. He says that this condition is much improved by the abdominal massage which he is obtaining at the Cornwallis Road Institution, but complains much of his nerves and is very emotional, but his reflexes are not exaggerated and there is no fibrillar twitching of the muscles of the face and tongue, nor any signs of physical deterioration due to psychasthenia. The pulse is slow, though regular, and equal at both wrists, and there are no signs of thickening of the arteries anywhere.
>
> He presents all the appearance of a very emotional man of the nervous type, but I am inclined to discount the possibility suggested by Dr Craig of a nervous breakdown.
>
> Internment to a man who has lived under the conditions under which Mr László has lived is of course a great hardship, but I do not anticipate any real danger to life or reason or a serious breakdown in health if the authorities consider it advisable that it should be continued.

At the request of the worried Mrs De László, reports were commissioned on him by his normal doctors, Dr Keightley and Dr Lund, as well as by Dr Maurice Craig, a 'nerve specialist'. Dr Keightley wrote:

> The lack of exercise and the condition of his liver tend to produce the alternate conditions of excitement and depression, and his whole constitution tends therefore to nerve fatigue.

If these conditions can be ameliorated, or he can obtain his release, I believe they will pass off under proper conditions otherwise it is quite possible that these mental conditions of excitement and depression may become permanent.

Dr Craig saw De László on 4 February 1918 and reported:

I find him in a restless condition; he is evidently getting loss of power of concentration; sleep is becoming defective; his circulation is bad, the pulse is slow and low tensioned, and he is losing weight.

The strain of the last few months has evidently told and is telling upon him, and if this restlessness continues, there is a grave danger of his having a mental breakdown.

I am of the opinion that it would be wise to let him have a ten grain dose of potassium bromide once a day, and if necessary he ought to be given a definite hypnotic. It would be wise for him to be in bed for a few weeks, but I do not know whether this is possible.

On 6 February Dr Lund sent a more worrying letter:

I saw Dr Keightley today and I find that he, Dr Craig and I all agreed to the risk, if not actual danger to your husband's mental condition by a prolongation of his present internment.

I have never seen him in such an unnerved state. His ordinarily highly strung mentality is suffering acutely under the strain of his present circumstances and life of inactivity, and I feel most strongly that it is running an unnecessary risk, and endangering his life by keeping him there.

The cumulative effect of the reports was to persuade the Home Office to allow him to be moved to a nursing home in Ladbroke Gardens, Notting Hill, and he was released there on

14 May 1918 having signed a promise not to go outside the home and its grounds or to communicate with anyone other than his wife. No doubt he was discreetly watched, but he seems to have kept his promise.

While De László languished in semi-captivity, events in the outside world began to shape in a way that was to have a profound influence on his future. There was still an intense feeling of hostility abroad in the country against aliens, perhaps unsurprising given it was the fourth year of a war that had been ghastly and expensive in terms of casualties and money. To most people it looked as though it was likely to extend well into 1919 or even beyond. There was also a lingering feeling that there were highly placed German sympathisers or dupes in the establishment who were deliberately sabotaging the war effort.

In May 1918 the eccentric and right wing MP Noel Pemberton Billing was sued for libel by the actress Maud Allan for alleging that her play *Salomé* was part of a German conspiracy to promote homosexuality and corrupt the manhood of Britain. He further alleged that there was a secret German list of 47,000 highly-placed British perverts who were being blackmailed into sabotaging the war effort. This was based on evidence that had been provided to him by an American named Harold Sherwood Spencer who had claimed British nationality because his grandparents were British and been commissioned into the Royal Irish Fusiliers in order to transfer to the Royal Flying Corps. On the basis of his speaking Albanian and a claim that he had spent time in the Balkans before the war, Spencer was sent to Italy to join the British Adriatic Mission where he served for some months in 1916.

It was Spencer's evidence that helped clinch the trial; he claimed to have seen the actual list, in the form of a 'Black Book', which was shown to him before the war by the German Prince Wied, who was king of Albania and to whom he had been a personal aide de camp. He had seen the names, their perversions and the means by which it was recommended the German Secret Service should approach them. He had passed the list, he said, to the British authorities who had suppressed it. The trial resulted in Pemberton Billing being acquitted of the charge of libel in a spectacular fashion after the jury deliberated for an hour and twenty-five minutes. There was a near riot in the court, with the gallery cheering and shouting 'Hurrah', and the ushers and police were directed to clear the court. A cheering crowd of a thousand people saw Pemberton Billing walk from the court and mobbed his car as he drove away.

Fortunately for Pemberton Billing and Harold Spencer, it was a civil case. MI5 and Special Branch had bulging files on Spencer going back to at least 1915. To them he was American, a journalist, a con merchant and sexual deviant with a tendency (that he was well aware of) to get over-excited and obsessive – not to mention delusional. In 1912 he had been arrested by the Italian police for assaulting a servant, and photographs were found in his suitcase 'of the sort whose mere possession is a criminal offence'. He had then attached himself to the US Embassy in Rome and claimed to be on the staff, but also claimed the ambassador was a Japanese spy. He had escaped from New York, leaving a litter of bounced cheques, in 1913 when his first wife was pressing charges 'of a serious nature', and returned to the Adriatic where he swindled the US Consul before proceeding to Albania. Though he claimed to have been confidentially employed by the Prince of Wied, MI5 thought it most likely that he had commanded an unofficial bodyguard in 1914.

Spencer appears to have done a good job while attached to the British Adriatic Mission: MI5 quietly expressed the opinion that they hoped he had not seen some of the letters from his superiors praising his abilities in a manner that was 'indiscreetly worded'. Whilst on leave in London he had done translation work for the Admiralty and was then, at some point, posted to his battalion in Salonika, which is when he seems to have flipped, telling all and sundry about German plots in London and claiming the Salonika intelligence officers were all under German influence. By mid-1917 he was raving; a medical board diagnosed delusional insanity. He started making allegations about scandalous sexual practices in the Asquith household and said of the British ambassador in Rome, Sir Rennell Rodd, that a 'Greek Jew financier' was blackmailing him because of his dedication of a volume of poems to Oscar Wilde thirty years before, with the result that the ambassador had been 'forced by pro-German influence to send away every intelligent member of his staff and replace them with others of conspicuous stupidity and incompetence'. He was soon found unfit and invalided out of the army, but found himself a job as an aeronautical inspector. He began to associate with Pemberton Billing and started writing for his *Vigilante* magazine. His evidence was purest fantasy but it helped bolster the festering feelings that not enough was being done against 'the enemy within'.

The anti-alien frenzy and concern about this secret internal enemy led the home secretary, Sir George Cave, to accept an amendment to his Nationality and Status of Aliens Bill of July 1918, which specifically stated that naturalisations which had taken place after the beginning of the war should be reviewed and might be subject to revocation. It was a pressing political point. In the Clapham by-election the Independent candidate (supported by Pemberton Billing's *Vigilante* magazine), Henry Hamilton Beamish, raised demands for the denaturalisation and internment of all former citizens of enemy countries in the United Kingdom, the closure of all foreign banks and the wearing of a badge by all foreign aliens. The Conservative candidate, Harry Greer, expressed the view that 'stronger measures' were necessary and published a letter from the prime minister who said he was 'determined to take whatever action is shown to be necessary'. Greer won with a reasonable majority, but given neither the Liberal nor Labour parties had put up candidates because of the coalition government, his opponent's 43 per cent share of the vote was worrying to the political establishment. The result of the amendment was that De László, along with every other alien who had been naturalised since August 1914, was required to have their status as British citizens examined and, if necessary, revoked.

The De László case had continued to fester and receive attention. Though the French Secret Service reports had received no mention in the press or the public hearing, the letter produced by Basil Thomson's agent mentioning Madame G and the forty reports allegedly submitted by De László was known about, if only vaguely. On 11 July 1918, Sir J.H. Dalziel, Liberal MP for Kirkcaldy Burghs, declared:

> You could almost have got a quorum of Members of the House of Commons who have been painted by László and who were able to say what an innocent person he was. It is very easy to be deceived, especially by enemy aliens. What was the case of Mr. László? He was found out, after a considerable time – it was kept a little bit of a mystery – committing an act of treason against this country, and, if I am not misinformed, just to show that you ought not always to trust enemy aliens, even though they have guarantees, *he was thanked, I understand, for his report on the condition of affairs in this country.* I only utter this to show that we really must not approach the consideration of this question full of trust in enemy aliens. I doubt not we have a duty to them. I am sure we have. But we have a duty to ourselves. Why should we take risks in time of war like we have been doing? No other country does it. Germany does not do it ... None of our Allies have shown the tenderness which we have up to the present.

In a debate on 15 April 1919, Sir Richard Cooper, Conservative member for Walsall, declared:

> De László was caught by the Government, in spite of the backing he had, from a letter which came from Hungary from his brother, in which his brother said he was instructed by the authorities to thank him for his fortieth report on the military situation in Great Britain ... What I ask is, Why was he not shot? If he had been a Britisher, and if it had been discovered that he had made a fortieth report on the military situation, I venture to think that he would have been shot by the most weak-minded Government that we could conceive. Why, then, was de László, who got the protection of persons in high places at the outset, when he was found guilty, not shot?

John Bull, the magazine owned by another right-wing populist MP, Horatio Bottomley, complaining about De László's treatment generally, reminded its readers that 'he was afterwards found in traitorous communication with the enemy – this "British" citizen who ought to have been court martialled and shot ... he used his position to worm out our military secrets and convey them by letter – nearly fifty of them – to the enemy'.

The Denaturalisation Hearing

FOLLOWING THE PASSAGE of the Nationality and Status of Aliens Act, the home secretary appointed a three-man committee to investigate and, where necessary, revoke the nationalities of all former aliens naturalised after 4 August 1914. Notices in the press instructed them to contact the committee directly by letter and requested members of the public with information also to send in their evidence in writing. Questionnaires were sent out to the individuals at the beginning of October 1918 asking for details of their relatives and property in formerly hostile states as well as when they last visited, whether they belonged to any clubs or associations linked to them, and whether any relatives had served in enemy forces. They were clearly designed to tease out former enemy aliens. Seven days were given to reply. Cases where naturalisation had occurred before the start of the war and there was suspicion of abuse were referred directly to the home secretary.

De László had, by now, been released from the nursing home following the intervention of some of his powerful friends and been allowed to live in the country house of his newly appointed solicitor, Sir Charles Russell, in Buckinghamshire. It can't be said that he didn't co-operate with the enquiry. As well as writing a personal defence, he wrote to Madame van Riemsdyk, to his family and to other persons he had been in contact with, authorising them to send, to the inquiry, his original letters. These were collected by the British Consul in Holland and by representatives of the Spanish government in Hungary and forwarded to the Foreign Office.

The authorities began to prepare their case against him, but ran straight into problems. A whole swathe of correspondence that had been used in support of their case before the internment committee had gone missing. The Treasury Solicitor noted:

> In August 1917 the Police searched the Holder's house and took possession of a number of letters and other documents. Certain of these were selected for use in support of the recommendation for internment, and are referred to in the report of MI5 dated 19th September 1917, being shortly described therein and lettered from M to Ze. Neither the documents themselves nor copies of them are attached to the report. On a perusal of the papers which came to me with my instructions, it became apparent that the documents mentioned would form an essential part of the case against the holder on the question of denaturalization, but, apart from this, as the case was likely to be strongly contested, it was clearly desirable that I should see and have in my possession all the documents which had passed into the hands of the Police.

To make matters worse, Charles Russell & Co., De László's solicitors, had applied to see them, which they were entitled to do. Despite a thorough search of the MI5 registry and of the Home Office, the documents never materialised. As the Treasury Solicitor pointed out, 'Messrs Charles Russell & Co may be expected to take full advantage of [this] on behalf of their client.'

Another problem concerned the French secret service reports, the most serious part of the case. The Treasury Solicitor pointed out:

> As matters stand, all we can do is to say that we had information that a letter in Hungarian, of which we have a French translation, was seen and the French translation taken. We can give no indication of the person who saw the letter or took the translation; nobody here is able to say that he knows who it was and is prepared to vouch for his trustworthiness.

He urged more effort be made to persuade the French authorities to let them give the committee a little more precise information about their agent and how he got the information. Presumably the French were obdurate, not wishing to give any clue as to even the existence of an important informant. In the end no mention was made of the reports, or of the letter obtained by Thomson's informant, in the charges levelled against De László.

The third problem involved the statements Thomson had gathered from some of De László's sitters. Though they had made written statements, they suddenly seem to have become coy about standing up in court to justify them. One was dead, which was about as coy as you can get, but Mrs Wanda Muller and Henry Vincent Higgins were still alive and presumably could not be persuaded to appear in court. It had been nearly two years since they made their statements but no real explanation appears on the file as to why they refused.

By the time De László appeared before it, the Revocation Committee, after a slow start, had been busy. Between 1 January and 31 March 1919, it revoked the naturalisation certificates of twenty-one former Germans, four former Austro-Hungarians, one former Turk and one former Russian. One of these cases, that of Caroline Hanemann, is worth looking at before examining the De László hearing in more detail. Caroline was naturalised on 13 October 1914. She had been born on 23 September 1857 in Nordheim in what was then the Duchy of Sachsen Meiningen. She was lady's maid and companion to Mrs Graham Smith to whom she also acted as a nurse because her mistress was an invalid. Mrs Graham Smith also happened to be the sister of Mr Asquith's wife. Being of German origin, Caroline had naturally come under suspicion, and an article in the magazine *The Pianomaker* in December 1917 made the allegation that she had actually resided within 10 Downing Street for a period round about 27 September 1916. Allegations were made about the 'Hidden Hand' that protected Germans and their friends, and about 'the sinister undercurrent of German influence' and the 'pampering of Huns'. The Downing Street story was probably true; Asquith frequently visited his sister-in-law in Easton Grey near Malmesbury and she sometimes visited him. MI5 had investigated the tale at the time and not discovered anything, though it did later receive a note claiming that Hanemann, at home in Wiltshire, had been found listening at keyholes, had opened and read her mistress's mail, and had openly expressed delight when news came through of German victories. All it could say about these allegations was that they were made by 'a responsible person in a position to know about what she was talking'.

Caroline appeared before the three-man committee at Westminster Hall on 21 October 1918. She went before it with no legal representation and called no witnesses. She answered its questions clearly and courteously, explaining her various positions before she took the job with Mrs Graham Smith in 1890. Mr Graham Smith had died in 1908. Both Caroline's parents had died before the war and she had three sisters and three brothers in Germany, with two nephews at the front in the German army, one discharged wounded and one exempt from service because of his health. She had last heard from the family the previous July and her communications had all gone through

Thomas Cook, a recognised intermediary. She had a sister who had also served as a maid, but she had returned to Germany in early 1915 when an attempt to obtain naturalisation had been rejected. Caroline had last visited Germany for ten days in 1912. When questioned about them, she explained what her male relatives did for work, all reasonable middle-class men with moderately responsible posts and all too old to have served in the war. The committee went through the various people who had supported her naturalisation application, all stalwarts of the local Wiltshire community, the teacher, the postmaster, the farm bailiff, Mr Lawson of the *Telegraph* who was a family friend, and Mrs Graham Smith herself. Mr Arbuthnot Lane, Mrs Graham Smith's doctor, wrote to support her because she had helped with Mrs Graham Smith's treatment.

Caroline explained her sympathies in the war lay with England and that it was a subject rarely spoken about in the house in front of her to save her feelings. All her money was in England and she was too old now to get any new work. She had done her bit in a small way for the war by making things for distressed folk and soldiers. When asked why she hadn't naturalised before the war she replied simply:

> Because I never thought about it. I never thought of a war; I never thought about such a thing. And then, I have travelled about a good deal in other countries, and I had no feeling – I felt rather cosmopolitan, I suppose you would say. I never thought. Then, of course, my lady is such an invalid, and she is so lonely and so dependent on me that I never felt that I wished to go away, of course.

She was thanked for her attendance and told she would hear the result through the Home Office.

They certainly took their time considering the matter. It wasn't until 6 February 1919 that the home secretary revoked the naturalisation, and not until the 16th that Wiltshire Constabulary was instructed to serve a copy on Caroline Hanemann. She became an Alien Enemy at that point.

Day One

The hearing to decide De László's naturalisation was held on 23 June 1919. Though the Armistice had been signed on 11 November 1918, the Versailles Treaty was still unsigned and, technically, the country was still at war. The Honourable Mr Justice Salter, a former Tory MP who had been a judge of the King's Bench Division, High Court, since 1917, was chairman. With him were The Right Honourable The Viscount Hambleden, Eton-educated and former colonel of the Devon Yeomanry, and His Honour Judge Radcliffe. The attorney-general Sir Gordon Hewart, KC, MP, Sir Archibald Bodkin and G.A.H. Brandon appeared for the Home Office, instructed by the Treasury Solicitor. De László was represented by the Right Honourable Sir John Simon, KC, a former attorney general and Home Secretary, Mr Harold Murphy, and Mr J. Wylie, instructed by his solicitors Messrs Charles Russell & Co.

The transcript of the five-day hearing runs to hundreds of pages, but, it has to be said, would run to an awful lot fewer without the verbiage spouted by both sides – in particular De László's defence barrister Sir John Simon. He seemed incapable of making any point without referring to the honesty of the police and the good will showed by the authorities in releasing all the paperwork, and in stressing that his client might technically be guilty, but … He repeatedly raised points but stressed he wasn't complaining on behalf of his client. A decade later, Oswald Mosley nicknamed him 'Soapy Simon', and it's quite plain here why.

De László himself appeared as a witness mainly to clarify some points on a written defence statement he had laid before the court. He was questioned surprisingly lightly despite his quoted desire that everything should be done in public 'in order that his real actions should be known, and that the gravity of the case should be put at its true weight'.

The case was widely reported in the press and the entire transcript is available in the files at Kew so the extracts quoted are purely the author's own.

The attorney general began by reminding the hearing of the terms of the British Nationality and Status of Aliens Act 1918, including the section which declared that if anyone to whom a naturalisation certificate had been granted 'has during the War in which His Majesty is engaged unlawfully traded with or communicated with the enemy or with the subject of an enemy state', the secretary of state should seek to revoke the certificate. The fundamental question was whether De László had done any or all of these things and then whether continuance of his certificate was conducive to the public good. He then gave basic details of the three charges – that De László had assisted the escapee Horn with money and had not informed the police for twenty-four hours, that he had, on numerous occasions, communicated through the Dutch diplomatic bag, and also that he had attempted to persuade Mr Winthrop Bowen to send letters to Hungary for him from New York.

He then set out the basic facts of De László's life including some details of his internment in 1917. He detailed some of the prominent persons he had painted including King George V, King Edward VII and Queen Alexandra, the Kaiser, President Roosevelt and the Emperor Franz Joseph. It was explained he had married Miss Guinness in 1900 and that, after living in Brittany, Budapest and Vienna, they had settled in London in 1907. He had, the attorney general conceded, 'a genius for portrait painting'.

Brooke Hughes

28 PATRICK ST.
CORK.

Vernon Kell in 'civvies' in 1904.

Barrister and MI5 officer Henry Honywood
Curtis-Bennett who sat in on De László's interrogation
and later worked for Basil Thomson at Scotland Yard.

The Old Bailey trial of German spy Carl Lody in October 1914 that resulted in him being shot in the Tower of London. Prosecuting Counsel (standing) is Archibald Bodkin, who also prosecuted in the De László denaturalisation hearing.

Assistant Commissioner Basil Thomson of
Scotland Yard who led the police investigation
and carried out De László's interrogations.

Headquarters of MI5 in 1915, Watergate House, York Buildings, Strand, known by the staff as 'Watertight House'.

Many MI5 officers had been wounded in the trenches but most retained their sense of humour about it!

THE VISIT OF D.C.I.G.S.
28. viii. 16.
D.C.I.G.S.: " And where were you wounded ?"
Capt. H. : " Oh, they knocked a piece out of my skull, so they sent me to the Intelligence Dept."

Our Mr. N. had occasion to enquire about one Laszlo, and was informed that he was " a high-class Portrait Painter."

(This is an entirely fancy sketch of this eminent artist by his humble follower.)

Portrait of a suspect as a street artist. Gladstone's tongue-in-cheek homage to a fellow artist. 'Our Mr. N.' refers to Robert Nathan, who was heading the early investigation.

Philip De László.

Philip De László.

15.xi.15. The latest Recruits.

Malcolm Brodie, Frederick Bosworth Booth and John Barr Fetherston, the three expert Post Office investigators, as portrayed by Gladstone when they formally joined MI5 in 1915.

'A Billet from Basil.' MI5 tended to think that Thomson was a bit too big for his boots and mocked his tendency to be unnecessarily mysterious.

Turning to the naturalisation itself, the attorney general said that in his defence statement De László offered four grounds for wishing to be naturalised: one was his marriage, one was his work, the third the similarity between the British and Hungarian constitutions and the fourth the traditional hospitality of Britain towards artists. He seemed to admit that there was evidence De László had had the intention of naturalising long before the start of the war, though he did point out that Britain had declared war on Austria-Hungary on 12 August 1914 and the application wasn't sent to the Home Office until three days later. The oath of allegiance wasn't sworn until 2 September.

The attorney general then read extracts of letters showing that the naturalisation had caused problems in Hungary, including the one that had been published in a Hungarian newspaper, and subsequently republished in the British newspaper *The Star*, which De László had written to his family saying, 'It has cost me a severe mental conflict, but on account of my five sons I had to do it.' The Hungarian newspaper commented he should be stripped of his Hungarian title and removed from the Hungarian Senate of Fine Art.

The attorney general and Sir John Simon traded quotes from the letters regarding the gifts of money sent to his family at some length before turning to the question of the correspondence being sent otherwise than through the post. Simon pointed out that De László had told the authorities about this, but the attorney general added darkly, 'there were other sources of information also' and De László had used 'a secret and unusual manner, namely through the Dutch Embassy Bag'. Madame van Riemsdyk's part was explained, as was her relationship with the Dutch foreign minister, as well as how Mrs De László had tried to get letters through Italy and how, following a letter from her to Madame van Riemsdyk bemoaning their difficulties, De László himself had written asking her to forward letters. Sir John Simon pointed out that these letters were sent through the normal post and the attorney general said he was merely showing how the use of the bag had eventually come about. He then produced a letter dated 13 October 1914 which contained a sentence, 'I send them open as they have to pass the censor here', which proved De László was aware of the censorship from early in the war. He then read a letter from Mr Winthrop Bowen in New York from January 1915 in which he said:

> By all means send me any letters you wish me to forward to the continent of Europe. Be sure and seal all letters and put them in a larger envelope … I will post them myself and not trust a servant to do it … just send me any letters you wish remailed.

Though there was later evidence that De László hadn't used this route, he said, it remained pertinent that he had considered it. Mail to the USA was not censored at that time.

The attorney general then turned back to Madame van Riemsdyk, explaining the usual method was to write to her enclosing a letter or postcard for forwarding and for her to then forward the replies and for De László to reimburse her. He read out a couple of her messages and Sir John Simon pointed out that one referred to the use of the diplomatic bag and both had been sent by postcard. The attorney general then read out a letter of 2 September 1915 in which van Riemsdyk explained that the size of the envelope was because she had received so much correspondence for him and the number of mail boats had been so reduced that she simply couldn't transmit them individually. Her brother had also put her under pressure to reduce the amount being sent in the bag so, she asked, could he request his people not to send so many letters? She added the line, referring to the letters to him, 'it would be no good my sending on the letters by post'. No one seemed able to explain *why* it wasn't possible to send them in the normal mail and, unfortunately, there was then an interruption in the flow of evidence when, with the permission of the president, the defence called Austen Chamberlain, chancellor of the exchequer, to give evidence of De László's character.

Chamberlain was giving evidence under subpoena (the only way a minister of the Crown could attend, though if he had been a private citizen he would have given evidence voluntarily), and it was asked whether he could give his evidence on the first day because of his extremely busy schedule. He explained, under questioning, that he had known De László for a number of years, that he had painted his portrait in 1913 and that they had had a number of friendly and open conversations. He was sure that the subject of naturalisation had come up during the sittings.

When asked about De László's attitude to Britain, Chamberlain said he had expressed a desire to get his sons into English public schools and that he had, indeed, helped him get the eldest into his alma mater, Rugby School. De László had also explained that, having lived in the freer atmosphere of Britain, it had become impossible for the couple to return to the more staid, oligarchic and narrow society of Vienna. As far as Chamberlain could tell, after the start of the war De László had held perfectly correct attitudes to the war as befitted a British subject, apart from an explicable hostility to the Roumanians that came naturally from his Hungarian origins. Apart from that, his attitude showed no sign of disaffection or hostility to His Majesty. On a more personal note he was quite happy to say that De László was a man of honour and that, 'it is inconceivable to me that he should take the oath of allegiance meaning to betray it or that he, having taken it, should betray it'.

In a brief cross-examination by the attorney general, Chamberlain admitted that he would certainly be one of the last people De László would be likely to admit to having other than utterly correct sentiments. He also said he did not recall any hostility being expressed towards the Serbians. After that, the witness was allowed to withdraw.

The hearing turned back to De László's correspondence via van Riemsdyk but the mysterious sentence saying letters could not be sent through the post was forgotten, the attorney general merely referring to the obviously large amount of material passing to and fro. He then referred to a postcard sent to Irma De László by Lucy De László dated 5 February 1915 but clearly sent via Van Riemdsyk as it was posted in Holland. It mentioned lack of recent contact (De László's mother was ill and he was clearly worried) and advised that they were off to Bath for the cure. He then went on to explain that, while in Bath, De László had sent the telegram which originally excited the attention of the authorities. Sir John Simon then went on to make a fuss about the telegram, claiming that there must have been a mistake, but that 'we are helping one another' so he would like to explain that De László had sent a previous one, when he had heard of his mother's death, and that this must have been the telegram referred to. He was, of course, quite incorrect, but he was to return to the subject later on.

The attorney general, quite confident he was talking about the correct telegram, stressed the importance of it, as the interview with Bath Police which followed was, quite clearly, a warning regarding communication with enemy countries. As he pointed out, however, De László was already aware there were problems because he had already acknowledged, in writing, that such correspondence was subject to censorship. In spite of this knowledge, both remittances and correspondence continued.

There was some difference of opinion on exactly when use of the diplomatic bag began, but it was certainly happening on 25 February 1915 when Madame van Riemsdyk wrote, 'I have asked my brother, the Minister, to send it to you through our Legation in London. It will not get lost there and I hope you will receive it without delay.' Further letters followed in June, specifically referring to mail being sent through the legation, and others in September and October, which included drawings for De László's mother's grave and one referring to the number of letters being sent in one packet. A letter from Daisy van Riemsdyk of February 1917 referred to Mr Ferdi Michaels acting as contact point for correspondence within the legation. The attorney general said he was quite unable to explain why some letters went through the ordinary mail and some were sent through the legation.

The attorney general then considered the Mayendorff incident, where De László had given him a cheque for £200 and asked him to transfer the money to his brother in Hungary. When originally questioned by the Metropolitan Police, De László had said that Mayendorff had owed him £1,000 for a portrait and had written to him asking to send £200 of the money to Hungary. He had, in fact, given Mayendorff a cheque in that amount and Mayendorff, it was clear from the correspondence, had made more than one attempt to send it. In Mayendorff's last letter the curious phrases 'to the address given' and 'to the person indicated' had been used rather than a proper address or a name. The attorney general pointed these out, asking at whose instigation these phrases had been employed.

When interviewed by the Met Police, De László had said his last remittance to Hungary had been in February 1916 and he had then discontinued sending money because he was told it was forbidden. It was clear he had sent further money by Mayendorff as a means of getting round the prohibition. The interview with the Met Police was clearly a second warning but, as the attorney general pointed out, 'no warning really is necessary. A British subject should know that such communications during war are unlawful … and nowhere does it appear that Mr De László consulted a solicitor or anyone at all.' There was considerable discussion over the number of transactions made abroad and the amounts sent, but it was clear De László had sent some £2,600 (£200,000 at contemporary values as calculated by the Bank of England inflation calculator) 'for the ultimate benefit of an enemy country'.

De László's correspondence then came under closer examination, as did his dealings with various Hungarians interned in Britain. These included De Weress and Czeisner, about whom De László had already been interrogated, but also a Hungarian woman with a sick son and an internee who had written to him and to whom he had sent £4. In his written statement he said it had never occurred to him that by giving this assistance it could lead to his loyalty being questioned. Examining De László's correspondence, the attorney general quoted extracts to show he had not lost his love of his native country. One correspondent wrote of 'your love for your romantic country' and Mr Guinness had written to him expressing his disapproval of De László's animosity to Russia (Britain's ally). The letter published in *The Star* was also quoted from, while in a letter of 11 March 1916 he had written to his sister expressing his pride in his nephews who were serving in the Austro-Hungarian army and in a later letter he had expressed the hope that his nephew would 'return victoriously'. In July 1915 he had written 'the beautiful feeling, for you, that you are doing your duty for your fatherland as a mother can console you, it is not permitted me, so I am doing it another way …'. Sir John Simon disputed some of the quotations, saying that because of the Austrian censorship De László was obliged to write in German, a language he spoke but did not write it well.

The attorney general turned next to the Horn incident. He read out Section 46a of DORA pointing out De László had broken it in two ways – by not giving information and by giving assistance in the form of money. He also mentioned what were, presumably, the two documents that Thomson's agent had discovered (MI5 had obtained more than two from the French and these could not be mentioned at all) and said that as far as this case went he placed no reliance upon them at all (they were 'copies of copies of documents'), but felt they should be mentioned as they supplied the starting point for other investigations. Copies were with the papers should the committee wish to see them. He then gave examples of previous cases relating to communicating and trading with the enemy, pointing out that by his own admission De László had done both on numerous occasions. He dwelt at length on the letters, pointing out that in none of the many of them was there any 'word, so far as I can see, of praise, or in the presence of blame, of exculpation of the country whose citizen he has become'. At heart, he suggested, De László remained Hungarian.

The first witness, Inspector William Marshfield of Bath City Police, was then called. He confirmed his identity and also that he had received a letter 'from a Department of the War Office known as MI5' (though in fact the letter must have been from MO5g) and that he had visited the hotel on 22 February 1915. He said he had not seen the original telegram but that the text was embodied in the letter from MI5. He had first checked De László's certificate of naturalisation and noted the date. He read him the telegram and asked if he was the sender. Marshfield asked why he had not sent it through the proper channels and De László said that it had concerned the death of his mother and that he had sent it this way 'because it would take a much longer time by any other route to send it'. De László had shown him various letters from prominent persons. He had reported the whole matter to MI5.

The president then asked a series of questions in reply to which Marshfield clarified that the issue was the sending of money to a neutral country (Holland) for onward transmission to an enemy country (Hungary), that the proper course was to send it direct by Thomas Cook (this was actually incorrect as Cook did not become the official intermediary until later, but an authorised intermediary had been required), and that De László, as far as he was concerned, seemed to know what the proper route was. Under cross-examination he repeated this point.

Matters then hung on the meaning of the telegram. Sir John Simon pointed out that it obviously referred to a previous message as no amount was quoted. He then mentioned a telegram of a few days earlier in which De László had transferred £200 to Holland and asked for the money to be transmitted to his brother – and also tried to arrange a meeting with Marczi László in Holland. Marshfield was, of course, unaware of any previous messages but he admitted the text made it appear so. He did state, however, that De László had not mentioned previous telegrams and neither had he. He said, 'Mr De László … produced a number of documents showing that he was a gentleman of high standing, and when he gave the explanation that it was with reference to his mother's death, I thought possibly that was correct.'

Sir John Simon then produced a long letter that Lucy De László had received from the family breaking the news of his mother's death and proceeded to read extracts to the court. Marshfield was asked whether he had been shown this particular letter and agreed, 'I might have been shown the letter, but I do not recall it.' He then withdrew.

Constable Isaac gave evidence that he had visited De László on 8 December 1916 and asked him if he had been sending money to his brother, receiving the answer yes. De László had said he had asked Baron Mayendorff to send him £200 from Madrid but had since found that this had not been done. He had previously sent money through van Riemsdyk, the last occasion being £500 in February previous. He had stopped sending money this way when told it was illegal. He had not been told to do anything about issuing warnings, only to obtain the facts. A slight discrepancy between what Isaac had noted and the dates on which money was sent was highlighted, in his usual unctuous fashion, by Sir John Simon ('I am not in the least doubting your complete good faith'), and Isaac promised to locate his pocket book, in which his first notes had been made. Then the witness withdrew.

Constable Allen of Kensington CID was called regarding De László's appearance at his station to tell him the whereabouts of Arpad Horn. Allen had, of course, kept notes and a copy of his later report. He said De László had provided him with a detailed description and shown him the envelope with 'Golden Cross Hotel' on it. The police had not known before this that Horn might be there. In a curious question, since it was surely one for the defence to ask, Bodkin enquired whether De László's information had contributed to the arrest and was answered 'Yes'. It was established that De László had reported the conversation with Horn outside the legally stipulated twenty-four-hour time limit and that there was an error in the date of the conversation as provided by De László in his statement.

The hearing ended for the day.

Day Two

Day two began with an agreement between prosecution and defence that there was no need for the policeman who had searched De László's house to be called as a witness. Sir John Simon, who throughout the whole day was tiresomely long-winded, apologetic, smarmy and insistent upon reading huge extracts from the correspondence, raised a point (though not a complaint) that some documents De László claimed had been removed had not been returned. The attorney general countered that the documents were there, in a box as yet unsearched by Sir John's team, who had been invited more than once to do so. As no complaint was pressed they moved on to the report of Mr Wyatt Williams and the two reports of the Advisory Committee on Internment, which were handed over to the court. Sir John Simon then moved on to De László's defence. He was, he said, going to claim that, whatever infringements of rules and regulations relating to correspondence there had been, his client had always acted with candour and openness when his attention had been called to them by the authorities. De László wished to claim that:

> … his errors, such as they are, were errors committed in good faith and that from beginning to end there is nothing in his conduct which is inconsistent with or was in any way a violation of the duty as he understood it, and he desires to continue to discharge it, of a British Subject.

He went on to explain, at length, that it was De László's wish for the hearing to be held in public 'in order that his real actions should be known, and that the gravity of the case should be put at its true weight'. He also wished it to be stressed that permission to have the case heard in public was not granted because his client 'holds a famous position in art, or because he is … a man of wealth and good connection'. The whole point of bringing the case in public was, he stressed:

> the most enormous contrast between the real extent and gravity of the materials which the Authorities offer for your consideration … and the terrible and dreadful rumours and whispers, not merely spoken from mouth to mouth, but actually published in some of our newspapers as to the case which the Crown has to make against this gentleman.

He stressed the enormous gulf between the supposed despicable conduct of 'worming out the secrets of this country and conveying them to an enemy' and breaches of the postal censorship and regulations to prevent money leaving the country. He and his client were not complaining about the 'restraint (internment), bitter, severe, undeserved in his conscience as he knows it to be' because they acknowledged that during wartime the authorities had to act upon accusations no matter 'how far-fetched the materials may be upon which they acted' and 'upon which we know, on reflection, no reliance is to be placed'. He reiterated that the committee was not there to enquire into the expediency of the internment order – it was there to decide whether, on the materials laid before them, De László (whose intentions to become naturalised before the war he laid on with a trowel) was an unfit person to remain a British citizen. The evidence of the Internment Committee was not relevant to this decision.

He then moved on to the point about De László sending money out of the country to Hungary. Apart from the visit by the Bath policeman, no attempt appeared to have been made to prevent other such transactions, even though the authorities knew of them. His open correspondence with Madame van Riemsdyk had clearly referred to it on a number of occasions; a letter from her was read out in which she clearly said, 'We have just heard from our Banker that his correspondent in Budapest had safely delivered the £200 to your brother.' The sentence appeared early in the letter (dated 3 March 1915) so was highly unlikely to have been missed by the censor. A postcard (not even in a sealed envelope) said, 'Dear De László – I have just received £200 from the Westminster Bank in your name, I shall forward it to your brother ...' and further pieces, not only from van Riemsdyk, which also quite clearly referred to money transfers to Vienna. While Simon didn't doubt that these were all in breach of the regulations he repeatedly stressed that if nothing was done about them, and his client had not received a clear instruction from the Bath inspector, how was he to know, in his own mind, that what he was doing was wrong:

> And if anything was calculated to make him suppose that the transmission in such circumstances as these, of such sums of money as these, to such recipients as these, by such means as these, was at any time objected to by the authorities, surely these letters and postcards were calculated to give him that assurance.

The fact that, of course, they were allowed to pass by MI5 in order to give him false assurance, in the hope of catching him in making a slip at a later date, is not referred to.

In the course of discussing the letters, it was touched upon that at least one had been sent via the Dutch diplomatic bag, and they moved on to this aspect of the case. A postcard dated 18 June 1915 clearly said, 'I am sending you letters from your brother through our Legation today. We received your telegram alright and forwarded the money yesterday morning to Lamar, as you requested us today.' As Sir John said, 'There you have both offences staring you in the face – money being sent out of the country, and the diplomatic bag being used for correspondence.' This was in June 1915. By reference to other letters he argued that there was no apparent system used to determine which correspondence was sent through the ordinary post or the bag, apart from Madame van Riemsdyk's wish to send some, more personal material, via a route that would be quicker. She, he said, made no distinction between the two routes. He produced further letters that had gone through the open post referring clearly to the transfer of money, and added, 'It was reasonable, it was perfectly reasonable for Mr De László to act down to that time on the assumption, in the belief, that what he was doing was unobjectionable.' He pointed out that

Mr Wyatt Williams, the accountant who had gone through the bank accounts for the Home Office, had made a similar point. He went on to say that Wyatt Williams had also cast doubt upon the nature of the warning given by the Bath police about the offence of sending money abroad in the manner it was being done. There had been, Wyatt Williams had concluded, confusion in De László's mind about the meaning of the telegram being discussed – he thought of it as being mainly concerned with correcting an earlier one he had sent arranging to meet his brother – and that the matter of sending money had not been understood. As a result, the money had continued to be sent. It's interesting, of course, that Inspector Marshfield hadn't thought this and that he had been the man who had issued the warning. Simon went on to argue that the Secret Service had construed the fact it had continued as something suspicious, but it was, he said, 'Nobody's fault, but it is a misunderstanding which, one is glad to think, has done nobody any harm, except, indeed, it has been the cause of a great deal of suspicion attached to Mr De László.'

Having gone over details of more of the transactions, Simon turned to the Mayendorff money. De László had been painting a portrait of the ambassador for some time and, when he visited London in September 1916, De László, who thought the main objection to his transfers abroad was that they depleted the monetary resources of Britain, had paid him £200 by cheque to be deposited in an account in Britain, with the money transmitted being sent from an account abroad. If it was a conspiracy, he said, De László had chosen a peculiar co-conspirator, an Allied diplomat 'whose good faith in the Allied cause no one impeaches'.

He then turned to why De László had stopped sending money. It wasn't because he had been visited by Mr Wyatt Williams, who visited long after he had stopped. He didn't do it because the authorities warned him. He didn't do it because his family was suddenly on a better financial footing. He did it because he had been told by his brother-in-law that it was wrong to send money out of the country. 'My Lord,' he said:

> I rely on this because it seems to me a very good test of Mr De László's good faith … How did he come to do it? What was the impelling cause which made him say: 'No, I must not do this any more'? It was the fact that he learned from his brother-in-law that it was not right and that was contrary to regulations to send money out of the country.

He then turned to the Horn affair and here he was blatantly inaccurate in his description of events. He admitted De László had given Horn a sovereign out of pity but then says that he had read in the newspaper that Horn was an escapee from Donington Hall and that had prompted him to go to the police. In fact he had known this from the start. So the tale Simon told of a penitent De László going to the police to admit his own error, while correct in some respects, was certainly not in others, yet it does not seem to have been challenged by the prosecution.

Simon then went on to point out that De László had, unprompted and while still interned, produced the long and detailed statement they had before them and that he had also gone out of his way to procure for them letters that he had sent abroad but not retained copies of. All this despite the fact that rumours were circulating that his letters were of a 'treacherous and improper sort'. He insisted on reading many of the letters that had been sent asking for the correspondence, a process that must have taken ages, eventually admitting the Crown had received them, dealt with them 'fully, fairly and faithfully' and translated them before handing copies to the defence. He went on to stress De László's loyalty to Britain, explaining some of his more apparently curious opinions on, for example, the Russians,

as being as a result of Hungarian history, not as a result of disloyalty, and challenged anyone to produce any statement De László
had made which threw doubt on his total loyalty to the state.

Simon then emphasised the importance, in wartime, of the
regulations De László had broken and acknowledged that he had
broken them, but then quoted the director of public prosecutions when he said, 'You have erred, but you have erred from a
noble motive.' He then proposed to examine De László's written
statement, but the president asked whether, among the letters
obtained from abroad, there were any which referred to money
transfer or use of the diplomatic bag. He also asked how often
the De Lászlós' wrote abroad using the normal post as opposed
to using the bag. Simon agreed to have them checked, but added
he was sure only five or six letters had gone in the bag so the rest
of the letters must have gone by the normal post. He then went
on to regale the committee about how De László had accidentally
overheard the Dutch minister discussing the British foreign secretary's displeasure at such use and how he had voluntarily stopped
doing so. The president also asked if the committee could be
told what the correct procedures were for both writing to enemy
countries and for the remittance of money.

Simon then began to go through De László's written statement, giving a potted biography and referring to his marriage
and the decision to move to London, and how his children were
growing up as English public schoolboys and he was looking
for a freehold property well before 1914. He also read the section where De László described his admiration for the British
constitution, which, he said, was rather like the Hungarian one.
In Austria there was an emperor, but in Hungary the same man
was a constitutional monarch and obliged, by law, not to speak
German while in the country. He was controlled by his min-
isters, who were all Hungarian, and by an elected parliament.
He was also attracted by England's fine artistic tradition in

portrait painting. In 1912 he had written to his brother saying he intended to naturalise as British and had told *Pall Mall* magazine too. In 1913 he had mentioned it to Lord Curzon as well as to Baron Forster, his great Hungarian patron. He really should have naturalised in 1913, but had been too wrapped up in his work. In 1914, before a hint of war, he had discussed it with Arthur Balfour and Mr Lee, who had volunteered to be a referee. On 13 June 1914 he had met his solicitor while out walking and asked him to commence work on naturalisation. This was before any hint of war. He had signed the application on 21 July and it was lodged with the Home Office on 28 July, over two weeks before Britain declared war on Austria-Hungary.

Sir John then turned to the letter published in *The Star* and demonstrated that the letter had been written in July 1914, not later as the authorities claimed. The Hungarian press had got hold of the letter from Marczi and used it to discredit De László, and the British press had simply followed suit. He went on to explain why De László had paid so much money to his relatives, detailing the family's circumstances and explaining how, over many years, he had been paying them remittances, mainly from his Austrian bank. The report from Mr Wyatt Williams had borne out De László's own assertion that the payments were regular and made to family members only. Simon went on to explain how Lucy De László had realised that the correct method of writing to an enemy country had been via a neutral one, and had written to Madame Colucci asking her to act as intermediary. He went on (having read all the letters virtually in their entirety) to stress that communications through Italy had obviously been quite legal and above suspicion.

Simon then asked that Lord Selborne be allowed to give his evidence as public engagements (though he was no longer a government minister) meant he could not attend later. This was granted, and Selborne said he had first met De László in 1910,

when he had painted his portrait, and that they had continued friendly relations ever since. During the sittings they had
discussed many subjects and 'Mr De László has the artistic tem-
perament very highly developed, and that at times led him to be
indiscreet in his opinions, and his expression of them.' He had
expressed himself particularly devoted to Hungary and the old
emperor Franz Joseph, but he had no love for Austria and a dislike of the Germans. 'He expressed his dislike of the Kaiser so
forcibly that he led one to think he was indiscreet.' De László's
attitude after the outbreak of war had not changed; he was capable of great indiscretion but incapable of anything dishonourable
or treacherous. He had always shown himself a man of great
honour and integrity, and Selborne could think of no reason
he should lose his citizenship. Cross-examined by Sir Archibald
Bodkin, Selborne did acknowledge that De László was devoted
to Hungary 'and that his devotion to that country seemed to be a
basic characteristic', but that he had often expressed his admiration for Britain and its institutions and said that his sons should
be brought up as English. He had no doubt that De László took
up his naturalisation without reservation and said that, as a
member of the government in 1916, he would not have asked
De László to paint a portrait of his son (recently killed in the war)
had he not been conscious of his integrity.

Following Lord Selborne's testimony, Sir John returned to
the subject of correspondence. He had sent letters to his brother
through Professor and Madame Colucci in Italy (then a neutral)
in 1914, but they had only been related to domestic matters.
Madame Colucci had written at De László's request before the
hearing and testified that the letters were perfectly ordinary
and had been sent unsealed so she could check them. He then
referred to the correspondence with Mr Winthrop Bowen
which reads, 'Yes. By all means send me any letters you wish
me to forward.' He pointed out that the route had never been

used and implied it was irrelevant. He then turned to Madame van Riemsdyk, stressing again and again (and again) that the bulk of the correspondence went through the ordinary post that was subject to the 'highly efficient and active examination of our military authorities'. He read out the letter by which the De Lászlós had been informed of the death of his mother – it was addressed to Lucy from the Hon. Mrs Charles Rothschild who had, herself, received the news from her sister who lived in Vienna. Mrs Rothschild said she wanted to break the news to Lucy personally so she could be the one to break it to her husband, but had been unable to do so because the De Lászlós had left town – hence the letter. Sir John then read out a further letter, received shortly afterwards, in which De László's sister-in-law Irma poignantly described Mrs De László's illness and death. He added, 'Is it not in the true sense a pathetic and tragic thing, that the intervention, quite right and proper, of the authorities should have broken in on this man at that moment of sorrow?' Inspector Marshfield had gone there to do his duty but, Sir John said, there was a misunderstanding:

> It was treated, and plainly treated, as a case where naturally the authorities wanted to know why he had been in communication with Hungary, what is it all about, it is my mother who is dying, here is the letter from Mrs Rothschild, read it; and the policeman goes away and naturally says that the man he interviewed was perfectly frank and candid …

De László, it was implied, had clearly misunderstood the nature of Marshfield's visit and that 'it was in these circumstances that he month by month with the greatest openness and greatest regularity by means of the ordinary post and under the very nose and eyes of the Authorities continues to send those sums to his relatives in Hungary'. No mention was made that Inspector

Marshfield had said in his evidence, quite clearly (and repeatedly), that in his opinion De László knew what the correct route for sending money should have been.

Sir John continued to labour the point, reading extracts from letters from February 1915 about the sending of money, and concluded, in his best 'Soapy' style:

> While I trust I would be the last to speak without fair consideration of the Authorities, one knows that they had a great deal to do, and very much more serious spies to follow than Mr De László. I am entitled, on Mr De László's part, to say: 'You really knew that in February 1915 I was sending £200 out of this country to Hungary. Why, if you please, did you not take some effective steps to stop me?' Instead of which, there follows, in March, £200; April, £100; May, £200; June, £300; July, £300; November, £300 and December £500.

He again stressed that the reason payments ceased was because De László received a warning from an unofficial source that it was illegal and promptly stopped. He then turned to the use of the Dutch bag. Towards the end of 1915, having used the normal post previously, De László became concerned that he had not heard from his family for some time and, fearing disaster, had telegraphed Madame van Riemsdyk. It was she who suggested he use the bag, as her brother, the Dutch minister for foreign affairs, had approved him doing so. She had, herself, used the bag to send him letters (including one which described the death of his mother), but was now suggesting he use it. Between then and August 1916, De László readily admitted sending six or eight letters via the bag, though each envelope may have contained more than one letter for his family. The letters were not individually enclosed in addressed envelopes so Madame van Riemsdyk could read them if she wished. Perhaps tellingly, Sir John was obliged to state that these envelopes were taken by hand and so did not pass through the postal system.

Sir John then explained, in detail, the money that De László had sent to his family through van Riemsdyk, including a dowry for his niece, and reminded the committee that he had stopped of his own accord when he was told it was wrong by his brother-in-law. On the matter of Baron Mayendorff he explained that De László had thought the problem with sending money abroad lay in the fact that it depleted the funds in Britain and so had given the baron a cheque for £200 on the understanding that the money be held or spent in London and a similar sum transmitted from abroad. He said that it was Mayendorff's idea to do this and that, of course, Mayendorff was a gentleman and one of Britain's allies. He rather cavalierly dismissed the phrase in Mayendorff's letter advising that the money transfer hadn't worked 'to the address given' and explained that, as far as could be discovered, the money had been returned to Mayendorff's bank and had never reached Hungary. He explained how De László had stopped using the diplomatic bag having heard Mr van Swinderen discussing the matter on the telephone, and produced the letter inviting De László to lunch that provided the date the conversation took place.

Sir John then turned to the interventions by the authorities following their 'discovery' of De László's behaviour (at least their discovery through overt sources, MI5 having, of course, been aware of them all the time). He explained how De László had co-operated thoroughly with the police officer from Paddington who had come to ask him about sending money to Hungary and claimed he had even told him about his use of the bag, though there is no mention of this in the statement DC Isaac made at the time. He had given full information to Mr Wyatt Williams and provided him with access to all his accounts and had happily signed an undertaking provided by the director of public prosecutions not to transmit more funds – though he had voluntarily ceased doing so long before.

The Horn incident was then described, though no one seemed to notice, or care, that here De László, in his written statement, seemed to contradict things he had said previously. Sir John read out the statement including the lines, concerning the initial letter presented by Horn's maid, 'I am here in great distress. I am a Reserve Officer of the Hungarian Army.' De László also admitted that, in the course of their conversation, Horn told him that he had been captured by the British while making his way home (presumably to take up his place in the Hungarian army) and had been interned ever since. Horn also told him, 'I am one of the three men who have escaped from internment.' The rest of the story followed the previous one – he had gone home, realised the seriousness of the situation, gone back to the studio next morning, had his maid find the torn-up envelope, done his morning sitting and then gone to the police. No one asked why he hadn't telephoned the police. It was held up as a shining example of De László's loyalty, and it was pointed out that the police would not have caught Horn without De László's intervention. It wasn't mentioned that Horn had had over twenty-four hours in which he might have escaped, and it was hardly to De László's credit that he hadn't.

Simon then read the portion of De László's statement relating to the letter Thomson had shown him and the allegations of spying:

> I believe this is only one of many silly slanders aimed at me, but even if there was any such paper I can only say that I have never been in touch, to my knowledge, with anyone connected with enemy secret service; but I would point out that an artist in my position is particularly liable to intrusion. I am bound, from the nature of things, to receive any person approaching me in the matter of my art, and I can readily see that the secret service of Germany might imagine that if they could gain access

to my studio they might meet persons there from whom news and gossip might be gathered. I have never seen the document referred to, nor has any charge been made against me relating to it; but if it does exist I, with all my strength, repudiate the inference which has been said to have been put upon it that I am in any way whatsoever in touch with enemy agents.

He went on to read De László's explanation of how his money in Hungary had been seized because he was a British subject and how, in Britain, he had been forced to suffer internment and to abandon his trade, leading to substantial losses. He said he had been subject to attacks in Parliament and to unsourced rumours that he was powerless to counter, which had done him irreparable harm. Since he moved to Britain in 1907 all his investments had been made there and he had invested £33,000 in war loans and £4,650 in Treasury securities. He had done work for the Red Cross and other funds, raising £4,500. He pleaded that revocation of his naturalisation would punish his wife and family. He did not wish to complain about his internment, which had been forced upon the authorities by feeling in England caused by Germany's conduct. He admitted that he had made mistakes but that his conscience was clear and he had never acted disloyally to the country of his adoption.

With De László due to give evidence the next day, there was some discussion of the legal points the committee wanted clearing up and the hearing adjourned to next morning.

Day Three

Day three of the hearing began with some remarks from Sir John Simon about De László's generosity towards his family, describing his kindness in helping his niece with her education and assisting his late mother. Simon agreed his motivation in sending money abroad 'would not in itself affect the rule and regulation which had been made to restrict the sending of money out of the country'. This didn't stop Simon from quoting, at considerable length, from several letters thanking De László for his kind assistance in a variety of matters, ending by saying, 'I think My Lord these extracts are quite to show what was the real character of the relation between this prosperous and famous artist and his more obscure relations in Hungary.' In other words, his generosity *was* something to be taken into account despite the rules and regulations.

He went on then to examine the business of the telegram sent from Bath in 1915. The attorney general had claimed that De László had been somewhat dishonest in his statement about the telegram by saying it related to the death of his mother. Quite simply, he said, the De Lászlós had been so overcome with grief they had misinterpreted the question and assumed he was talking about a telegram they had sent a few days earlier, which actually did refer to the chance of a meeting in Holland to discuss his mother's death. Quoting extensively from the report of Mr Wyatt Williams, the Home Office inspector, he pointed out that Williams had noted the original telegram and had himself deduced that there had been confusion between the two. Again, no mention was made of Inspector Marshfield (who had carried out the interview) and the fact that he had said quite clearly (and repeated) that in his opinion De László knew what the correct route for sending money should have been.

Simon then turned to the correspondence abroad. It was clear from an analysis of the letters, he said, that all outgoing letters between August 1914 and the end of 1915 had gone out in the normal mail, under the eyes of the censors. It was only for a period of about five months that, at Madame van Riemsdyk's suggestion, the Dutch diplomatic bag was used to send letters abroad and then only on five or six occasions (he forgot to mention De László had said six or eight). As soon as he had discovered, by accident, that the foreign secretary disapproved of this, De László had voluntarily stopped. He then went through some of the letters and pointed out that one of them stamped as having been 'Passed by Censor' made explicit reference to Madame van Riemsdyk acting as intermediary for letters to Baron Forster (though he seems to have forgotten that this could be perfectly legal if done correctly). He also read out some of the letters to the family, known to have passed through the bag, emphasising their perfectly harmless nature. He then pointed out that the undertaking that the director of public prosecutions had made De László sign made no mention at all of communicating with his relatives, merely committing him not to send any more money to them, even though the authorities were perfectly aware that he had been writing to them.

Simon then read some of the correspondence with Baron Forster, pointing out that it dealt only with family matters, and queried a previous comment that it contained nothing favourable about Britain, his adopted country, pointing out that it would have to pass through enemy censorship so it was wise to restrict the contents. He did point out one, probably erroneous, pro-British piece of propaganda that De László had sent. On the back of a newspaper clipping about some work he had done raising funds for the Red Cross had appeared an article on how well captured Zeppelin crews were treated – this at a time when German propaganda was saying exactly the opposite.

Simon then went on at some length to point out that the legislation under which the committee was sitting did not automatically remove citizenship from someone who was found to have breached the defence regulations but that it was for the committee to decide whether it was in the national interest for them to do so, adding that he hoped De László's noble motives in transgressing would be taken into account and that 'to be inspired by an upright and noble motive and to admit your errors, these my lord, are among the qualities which we would be proud to associate our own civilization'.

Mr Herbert Ernest Fass, a first-class clerk at the Treasury, was called next. On being questioned about regulations on sending money to enemy territory he said the rules for Austria-Hungary were more lenient than those for Germany but that as far as he knew no permission had ever been granted (except in the case of a few Austro-Hungarians who had been interned) for remittances to family members who were not of British descent. The usual amount of a monthly remittance would have been about £10, and this was only allowed where a case of real hardship could be shown. All money had to be sent through a recognised intermediary. Sir John Simon, cross-examining, asked whether, assuming the correct authority had been received, the sister of the Dutch foreign minister would be acceptable, and received the answer yes. It was established that, in 1915, use of Thomas Cook as an intermediary was only advised, not mandatory, and was mainly for the convenience of the censor. It was established that the censorship people knew the rules about transmitting money and that no letters from or to De László mentioning such transmissions had ever been received by Fass or his Treasury department. In addition, though the rules were interpreted strictly, there was a certain amount of leniency granted to Austria-Hungary, in part because of its treatment of Britons trapped there.

Simon stated that part of the defence was based on the fact that the censorship was under the control of the military and that it had allowed letters to pass, and Fass agreed, at least to the point of acknowledging the censorship was under military control. When pushed, Fass agreed reluctantly that sending money abroad to relatives was 'trading with the enemy' only in as much as it was covered by the Trading with the Enemy proclamation.

Re-examined by Sir Archibald Bodkin, Fass agreed no one could send money abroad without the necessary authority. Bodkin asked him about the efficiency of the censorship, pointing out it was a large organisation which employed 'masses' of women, and Fass agreed that he knew of cases where errors had occurred and letters had been overlooked. Bodkin pointed out that the three postcards Simon had shown him were dated two or three weeks apart and said that it was quite likely that each would have been examined by a different person so might have slipped through. The president then asked about the terms of the proclamation and where people might find out about them. Bodkin pointed out that the proclamation explaining who to approach was on the walls of every public building. Fass did agree that, in most cases, the method was brought to the attention of individuals by the censorship when it caught people breaking the rules, giving Simon the opportunity to point out that this had never happened to De László.

The next witness was Adrienne van Riemsdyk, who confirmed her name, address and that her husband was head of the archives at The Hague and her brother the foreign minister. She had known De László for ten or twelve years; he had painted members of her family and they had become great friends. Her daughter Daisy, who referred to De László as 'uncle', had married a British officer. Simon produced letters from the De Lászlós from early in the war (which she had voluntarily sent to England for the committee) in which it was specifically mentioned that enclosed letters to the family were sent 'open' as they had to pass the censorship. Some of the early ones she had forwarded to Hungary in the diplomatic bag. She had done this on her own initiative and had later suggested to the De Lászlós that they use the same method. All the early letters had come through the ordinary post and she hadn't read them because they had been censored. They were always

marked as having been opened. On being questioned, she said
the letters were written in German and agreed that De László's
German was eccentric.

After a while, one or other of the De Lászlós had expressed
concern about letters being delayed or going missing and she had
suggested using the bag. She had consulted her brother, who was
reluctant but had agreed on the basis that she read the letters and
act as censor! Though it was unpleasant reading private letters she
had done so (with the exception of the letter about his mother's
death which she had merely glanced at out of respect), and none
contained anything but family matters. She had sent a letter to
London relating to De László's mother's illness through the bag
for the first time because of its importance.

Various letters were then examined to try and establish which
might have arrived in the bag and which by normal mail before
the questions moved on to transmission of money. Sir John
Simon went through the normal method of payment – De
László would send a draft on his London account with London
and Westminster Bank to her, which she would cash and then
send a draft from her bank to Hungary. De László would write
to her through the normal post telling her and she would reply
in the same way, usually quoting the amount sent. She had
never thought there was anything wrong in doing it and would
have stopped if she had. She was puzzled when the payments
ceased. She had written about money via the bag on at least one
occasion, when she had received a large sum of money but no
instruction on where it was to be forwarded to and presumed
the letter had been mislaid in the normal mail. She was aware
that other people were trying to use the bag for private correspondence and had written to De László at one point asking
him to request his family not to send so many letters for her to
forward as it might cause a problem for her brother. She never,
she said, concealed treacherous correspondence for anyone.

When asked, Adrienne said she knew the Dutch minister in London, Mr van Swinderen, very well. Between January and July 1916 she had received four or five letters from De László via the bag and she believed she had told him to approach van Swinderen about doing so. No one in Holland had complained about the practice and she didn't know why he ceased using the bag and reverted to the normal mail.

On cross-examination by Sir Archibald Bodkin, Madame van Riemsdyk insisted that she had suggested being the postbox for the De Lászlós but was challenged with two letters, one sent by Lucy De László in which she mentioned their attempt to send letters via Italy, and one from De László himself in which he 'took the liberty' of enclosing two letters for her to forward. It was only when presented with this letter, and the fact that no correspondence from her suggesting she be used as an intermediary could be found, that she admitted the original idea came from De László. She continued to say that it was her idea to act as intermediary for letters from the family, although no correspondence could be found for that. She said forwarding the letters by 'special courier' was the first time she had used a diplomatic bag and that she had checked with her brother and he had asked her to read and censor them. She didn't check the letters from his family because they had been cleared by the Austrian censor, but put them in a fresh envelope addressed to London and expected the British censor to check them. She only read material that came via the bag.

Madame van Riemsdyk said she had sent by bag, and had thus read, a letter from the family that she accompanied with a note to De László saying, 'I trust you have good news now and feel happy again about your loved ones.' Why ask that question, said Bodkin, if you had read the letters and knew their content? She insisted she read them all properly rather than just skimming through them. When another letter was produced using a similar phrase regarding the contents, she was again probed about whether she actually read them. She insisted she did, but included such phrases as a means of disguising the fact, as she didn't want De László to know she did so.

Madame van Riemsdyk was asked if she had ever met De László's brother Marczi (the answer being no), and whether she knew he was liable to be called up, to which she replied that she knew, from the letters, that it was possible. She was given a letter from De László dated 7 September 1915 and asked to read the first line, which she translated as, 'Thank you for the good news and also for the news about Harkanczi, I am happy with his friendship. I am pleased but do not want to make more use of his friendship.' She said, however, that it might have implied De László did not want to abuse the friendship. When Simon complained she was being asked to translate, Bodkin snapped, 'She knows both languages.' She admitted that she did not know who Harkanczi was – she certainly didn't know he was a Hungarian officer named Jason Harkanczi. She did not recall any letters in which De László had asked Harkanczi to use his influence to keep Marczi on home service and away from the front, prompting Bodkin to say that the reason she didn't remember the contents was because she never read them, which she denied.

Bodkin then asked about her procedure when the letters arrived; she had struggled somewhat with the translation and had earlier said she sent them on the same day. Bodkin said, 'So that when the post came in you sat down to read them and decipher (he was referring to De László's handwriting) them, and translate them to yourself and send them on the same day?' She agreed that this is what she did. He then asked to refer to another letter in which Marczi mentioned a letter from his brother to Harkanczi and another to Baron Forster. Did she remember any letters to Harkanczi or any such name? The answer was no, but she did remember letters, two or three, to Forster. She was asked whether she knew when De László stopped using the diplomatic bag and was unable to provide a date, though she had continued to use it until he was interned. De László had never asked her to stop using the bag or explained why he had stopped. She had continued to use the bag long after he had stopped. Bodkin produced a letter from Daisy van Riemsdyk dated 25 May 1915 in which she said, 'Mother will certainly ask my Uncle about the forwarding of the letters.' What did this mean? She was quite unable to assist.

She was asked about the transmission of money to Hungary but was incredibly vague about the actual mechanics of it – her husband seemed to have dealt with the onward transmission to Hungary once the money arrived in a Dutch bank from London. She knew, she said, that the money was going to Hungary but, when pressed, said she hadn't thought it odd that money was being sent from Britain to a country with whom she was at war. She had never spoken to her brother about it or taken advice. 'It seemed quite natural to me, because it was sent to relatives who wanted the money.' Asked how she knew they wanted money, she said she knew it from their letters. Bodkin pointed out that none of the letters asked for any, to which she said, 'They did not say they were in want of money, but I made out from Mr De László's letters that he liked to make presents because he thought they wanted money. They did not ask for it.' She did remember a letter from Hungary asking not to send any more, but had continued to send it on when De László asked her because it was none of her business.

Asked whether De László was the only person for whom she acted as forwarding agent, she said yes. She was quite sure of this. She was also quite sure he was the only person for whom she used the privilege of the diplomatic bag. She was then asked if she knew an address in Schloss Liblin, Austria-Hungary, and recalled it was the address for an Englishman to whom she forwarded post on behalf of his mother in England. She knew neither the Englishman nor his mother but had been asked to act by friends. The letters were in English and she forwarded them openly. She didn't deal with any others. The letters and postcards out of Austria were from an Englishman, Victor Farrell, and there were two letters to him from his mother. These were perfectly legal.

After a few trivial questions, Madame van Riemsdyk withdrew.

After some discussion about the number of witnesses Sir John Simon planned to call (many) and the timing of the committee going forward (one committee member had a public engagement on Saturday and the president had to be in Liverpool on the Monday), Philip De László was finally called to be examined by Sir John Simon on some points relating to his statement that Sir John had already gone through, at length, in his opening speech.

First of all Sir John turned to some small slips that had been made in De László's printed statement, which he had drawn up in November 1918, and which had been presented to the committee. There was an error regarding the number of transactions that was easily cleared up, an error with the date of his second police interview (the one with Isaac), and a day's error in the date of the Horn incident which might have made it appear he had waited two days before going to the police. They were sorted out quickly. Apart from those, the statement was correct.

Simon took him through the Horn incident in some detail, establishing that, though it was over twenty-four hours before he went to the police, it was only twenty-four-and-a-half hours. He then turned to the individual charges. Had he ever felt or shown any disaffection or disloyalty towards His Majesty? Answer: no. He did not think that the severe mental conflict he had mentioned in the letter reprinted in *The Star* was inconsistent with his loyalty. The date of the letter was definitely 27 July 1914 and not as late as November 1914 as the authorities had appeared to think. The committee was reminded that war was not declared between Britain and Austria until 12 August, and a great deal of time was spent discussing the process of naturalisation and the timescales involved. Sir John pointed out that all naturalisations were investigated by 'the Secret Service Department of Scotland Yard' (actually by Special Branch, which usually just checked for a criminal record for the applicant and referees and made some desultory enquiries locally).

The press campaign in Hungary to have De László stripped of his title and his work classed as 'foreign' was gone over and De László assured the committee that he had had nothing to do with releasing the letter that had later appeared in *The Star.* De László explained he had specifically mentioned his five sons as being a reason for naturalisation as it would inspire sympathy among his own family. His sons were talked about; they had been brought up as British and had attended public schools. His eldest son had just finished at Rugby School, was applying to join the army and had been doing 'war work' in his holidays with the knowledge of 'the authorities'. He also played football! His brothers were also true British schoolboys.

Sir John then turned to the two interrogations at Scotland Yard, saying it wouldn't be proper to name all the persons who had been present. The interrogation transcript had only recently been released to De László and his legal representatives, and it was the first time De László had actually seen it. He had been asked about the letter in *The Star* and denied that he had written it. 'At the time that you gave that answer were you endeavouring to answer accurately?' Sir John asked. De László replied, 'I tried to do my best. I must have forgotten it.' He went on, 'It was an honest mistake. I was overwhelmed.' The interviewer had claimed that the letter was written in November 1914, prompting the response that he could not have written it then because he was sending correspondence through the Dutch Legation and someone might have seen it 'and gone home and told lies about it'. Mention of the Dutch bag had apparently created the impression that the letter had been written in wartime, said Sir John, something that was vehemently denied.

The questioning then turned to the two witnesses who had given statements about De László's behaviour in his studio, neither of whom were presented to the committee. No explanation for their non-appearance was given, but it gave De László the opportunity to say he had never spoken in a disloyal or disaffected way to any man or woman. It then turned to 'trading with the enemy'. It was clear, said Sir John, from one of his letters, that De László knew that his mail might be censored. Had he, at any time, been warned by the censorship about sending money to Hungary? 'Never', came the reply. It was only when he mentioned it casually to his brother-in-law that he realised it was wrong and stopped doing it. 'So you were ultimately restrained, not by the vigilance of the authorities but by learning what the position was from your brother-in-law?' 'Yes, that is so.' He had assumed that rule actually applied to sending money out of the country, which was why he had given Baron Mayendorff a cheque to be paid into a British account and the money transferred from an account abroad. He wouldn't have done it if he thought it was wrong.

Next came the business of using the diplomatic bag. De László was asked, 'If you get a letter which has come through the Dutch Diplomatic Bag to the Dutch Embassy here in London, and it is sent to you by the ordinary post, have you any idea what you ought to do with it except receive it?' He responded, 'No, I received it and never gave it any thought.' Regarding the use of the bag out of the country he said that Madame van Riemsdyk had suggested it; he had used it only four or five times. Sir John produced a telegram and a copy letter from Mr van Swinderen referring to an invitation for De László to visit him for lunch on 3 August 1916. He had gone to the embassy on that day and overheard van Swinderen talking on the telephone and saying to the person on the other end, 'I cannot forward any letters more for you as Sir Edward Grey does not like it, he told me about it and I do not want to do it any more.' The message was not intended for De László but he had overheard it and van Swinderen had said, on putting the phone down, 'I am so sorry, people bother me constantly for sending letters and I am tired and I do not want to do it more.' De László had immediately told van Swinderen he did not want to use the bag himself now, but van Swinderen had, apparently, said he would continue to do so. De László himself had refused this offer because 'it is not the right thing to do'.

The hearing was adjourned.

Day Four

Day four began with Sir John Simon saying he had dealt enough with the letters via Madame van Riemsdyk. He turned instead to those that had been passed to Hungary via Italy early in the war. On 17 August 1914 Lucy de László had written to Mrs Colucci in the then neutral Italy asking if she, as a neutral, would forward correspondence. Mrs Colucci had agreed and two letters had been forwarded by her. Under questioning, De László said he had known of Dr Colucci, who was an editor of the Italian art magazine *Vita d'Arte*, since 1909 when they had corresponded, but that he had never met him. He and Lucy had, however, met Mrs Colucci on a visit to Siena in early 1914. Led by his counsel, De László admitted that during his interrogation he had completely forgotten about Colucci – hence the confusion about Italy and a letter to someone whose name began with C. It was only when he returned home and saw a copy of *Vita d'Arte* that he remembered him and the letter. Lucy had written to Basil Thomson enclosing a copy of the magazine and explaining everything; unfortunately the attorney general was unable to produce them and a search was instituted.

Sir John then turned to De László's arrest. It was explained who arrested him and when, that the police were waiting also at his studio and how he had been taken to Scotland Yard after handing over his keys. In typical 'Soapy Simon' style he described the detectives' search as 'An unpleasant experience and I have no doubt done with the thoroughness which is habitual with the London police.' He then explained the schedule of interrogations De László had been subjected to and began to ask about the questions relating to the Horn incident. They went through the questions and answers at length, and De László agreed that he had given a full and honest account of events.

Sir John then mentioned the next question, about whether De László had lots of relatives in Hungary (to which De László had answered, 'Yes, I still correspond with them through Holland. I have a brother and two sisters with whom I correspond') and asked whether he had realised at the time that virtually the whole of his correspondence was passing under the eyes of the police – apart from the few letters that had gone through the Dutch bag. De László said he had absolutely no idea about this (which seems a little peculiar given that his latest biographer, working from his personal papers, suggests otherwise), leading Sir John to say, 'A great many people think our secret service is not nearly as good as it really is', adding that every letter De László received and sent was being opened, which he asked the attorney general to confirm.

Mr Justice Salter asked De László if he was aware of censorship generally, to which he replied yes, he had received letters marked 'Opened by Censor', but Sir John wanted to know more about the special supervision of the correspondence, which he knew involved letters being opened secretly and resealed. The attorney general was forced to concede that all correspondence to

De László's address was secretly opened ('including Mrs László and, perhaps, the servants') and that it was done by special order. Mentioning Mrs van Riemsdyk's previous testimony, Sir John asked specifically whether MI5 (he actually named the organisation) had opened and examined all the correspondence between her and De László. He then proceeded to go through the interview transcript in detail, pointing out where, in retrospect, it was obvious that Basil Thomson's questions were based on the correspondence that had secretly been read. He asked for copies of some of the correspondence to Madame van Riemsdyk, in particular the first letter sent by Lucy specifically requesting that no more correspondence be sent through the diplomatic bag. Unfortunately the attorney general was unable to produce them and Basil Thomson, who was observing the proceedings, had to be questioned (not publicly) about his recollection of the interview, though he couldn't confirm exactly what correspondence he had had in front of him during the questioning. The loss of some of the evidence between the Home Office, MI5 and the Treasury solicitors was quietly played upon by Sir John and possibly influenced unfavourably the committee's opinion of the efficiency of the investigators.

Sir John went through the interview sentence by sentence until Mr Justice Salter, in some exasperation it seems, interjected:

> Sir John Simon, what is the good of going through this long and very proper roving enquiry to which Mr László was subjected at Scotland Yard? Considering the danger in which the country then stood one is glad to find how diligent the authorities were … I do not see quite how it helps us. The Crown have put on a piece of paper matters which they suggest to us we should enquire into and we are supposed to go into them. We do not care what questions Sir Basil Thomson put at all … I do not see what useful purpose is served by going through all this.

They had been hoping to get the enquiry over by the end of the day. Following a grovelling apology, Simon finally explained the purpose of his long series of questions – that he wanted to stress that the authorities knew all about De László's sending money abroad and that his claim to retain his British citizenship rested on the fact he had been tested in the very strongest way already in the interrogations and not failed. After further apology he turned to the question of De László's basic loyalty. Could he state in one sentence his feelings towards Britain and her intervention in the war? De László answered succinctly, 'It was the bounden duty of England to come into this war.' He was asked about Italy, which had reneged on its alliance with Germany and Austria-Hungary and attacked Austria, and said he was in favour of its intervention because its intent was to unite all Italian speakers. He did admit to having had bad feelings about the Russian alliance, in part because of Hungary's long antagonism, but swore he had never said or done anything that was disloyal or disaffected towards the British Crown.

The attorney general then examined Mr De László. He expressed surprise that he had said he had no suspicion Basil Thomson knew about his correspondence. He had been visited by the police over his letters regarding Mayendorff and he also knew Mr Wyatt Williams had been through his correspondence in detail. He also pointed out that, in the course of the interview, De László had actually said, 'I take it for granted that you know everything about me.' He was also forced to admit that Thomson must surely have known about those matters that he had been warned about by the director of public prosecutions. He then turned to the matter of the naturalisation. De László agreed he had lived in London since 1907 and said that he had first instructed his solicitor to start the procedure on 13 July 1914, though he said he had made up his mind to do so in 1912 or 1913 – indeed he had told Baron Forster about it in 1913. When confronted by the grounds upon which he had asked to be naturalised (which were on the application memorial as 'from a desire to continue and improve said business as an artist, so as to attain an honourable independence from such business, and to provide for his future years and sustenance'), he expressed amazement as he was quite clear, he said, that one of the chief reasons for his desire to become British was for the sake of his sons. It was pointed out that he had signed the memorial and taken an oath on it, and that it was the only ground upon which his naturalisation was based.

The questioning then turned to the Hungarian reaction to De László's naturalisation. The attorney general referred to the letter that was reprinted in *The Star* newspaper, which De László agreed he must have written, though he quibbled somewhat about the exact translation. He did agree that, in general terms, it expressed his feeling at the time. Other letters were produced in which he had stated that it was on account of his sons that he had naturalised, and he conceded that they were one of his main reasons for doing so. When asked whether he had delayed naturalisation out of esteem for Emperor Franz Joseph he agreed that was the case, but that this was merely a postponement of the action. When he had been questioned by Thomson about the letter and denied writing it, it was because he was confused by so many questions. He denied ever having said that he might have wanted to recover his Hungarian nationality and denied, under close questioning, that he had helped Arpad Horn because he was Hungarian, but could not deny having told Thomson that he had not given Horn up immediately because he was worried about Hungarian opinion of him after the war. Was there, he was asked, a conflict between his duty as a British subject and his sentiment towards Hungary? De László's reply was that his main concern was in giving up another man at all, regardless of nationality.

De László was then asked whether it was more important to him that the war ended quickly or that Britain won. He replied that Britain winning was most important, but was then questioned about his letter of July 1915 in which he had expressed the hope that his nephew would return from the war 'victoriously'. This, he replied, was to help shield his unhappy sister and to offer her hope. 'I wanted to say something nice to her, which would appeal to her from her point of view, as a mother of her only child.' There was much discussion about the exact wording of the letter as, De László admitted, his German was not perfect. Though the word he used, *seigereich*, meant victorious, it could also, De László argued, mean successful. He admitted he had never lost all feeling for the land of his birth but denied the war had intensified his feelings towards it. Various letters to his sister were read out in which De László described his two nephews, in the Hungarian army, as 'heroes', sent money which he admitted would be used to help them and referred to meeting his family again in 'the hour of delivery'. He was quite unable, when prompted by the attorney general, to point out any mention in any of his letters of his gratitude to, affection for or appreciation of, England.

The attorney general then turned to the use of the Dutch bag, forcing De László to say that he thought its use commenced 'at the end of 1915'. The attorney general then produced a letter dated 25 March 1915 in which Madame van Riemsdyk's daughter clearly said (to Mrs De László), 'Mother will certainly ask my uncle about the forwarding of the letters' and another, from van Riemsdyk herself, dated 14 June 1915, which said, 'I am sending this through our Legation – it is the safest way – as we do not write secrets.' A further letter, dated 18 June 1915, again clearly referred to the use of the bag. De László was reminded that in his interview with Thomson in August 1917 he had clearly said that use of the bag began 'at the beginning of last year', i.e. 1916. When pressed he admitted that he had also told Thomson that Madame van Riemsdyk had suggested it in a letter, though no such letter actually existed. He did stress that he had only sent four, at the most five, letters through the bag, but was quite unable to say how many he had received that way. His wife, he knew, had destroyed some. As far as he was concerned he had definitely ceased to send letters that way on 3 August 1916, but admitted that he had continued to receive them after that date.

The attorney general interrupted him to refer to a letter from Madame van Riemsdyk dated 2 September 1916 in which she said, 'Do not start at the size of this envelope. I have received so many letters for you during the last days that I could not possibly send them all as they came in.' She asked him to request that his family send fewer letters, but promised to continue sending his letters out that way. An excerpt from a letter from her, dated 7 May 1917, was read out, and it was pointed out that the letter was carrying a London stamp and postmark, proof that it had entered the country via the bag. When it was put to De László that he had been made aware that use of the bag was frowned upon on 3 August 1916, he said that he had not considered whether there was a problem with her continuing to use it, adding, 'Both our consciences are clear. We did nothing wrong.' When asked why, if there wasn't a problem he had asked her not to use the bag herself, he said this was after his interview with the director of public prosecutions: 'after I had all this complication and unpleasantness I must have asked my wife to write to Madame van Riemsdyk not to send because they do not like it here.' When it was pointed out that in her evidence Madame van Riemsdyk had denied receiving any request to stop using the bag, De László was able to score one point – he told the attorney general that he had seen a copy of his wife's letter requesting exactly that at his interview with Thomson!

The attorney general then turned to the question of De László's knowledge of the rights and wrongs of using the bag. Did censorship ever come to mind while he was doing it? De László denied this, but a letter he had written in October 1914 was produced in which he had referred clearly to censorship. He was then asked about an attempt to get a letter through to Sweden without going through censorship. This he declined to answer because it was, apparently, an effort made by his wife to use her maid as a courier that he had only recently found out about. He was reminded that he had communicated through Italy and through Switzerland, and admitted he had sent a postcard to Baron Mayendorff in Madrid via the American ambassador as well as having written to Mr Winthrop Bowen enquiring about using him as a means of forwarding letters. He was certainly well aware of the rules about censorship and use of the mail generally.

They then turned to the Bath Police visit in 1915. De László denied point blank that he had been issued any warning by Inspector Marshfield (despite Marshfield's statement). After many interruptions from 'Soapy Simon', the president said, 'It was not a warning against sending money, but it might have been to some extent a warning. At any rate the policeman thought the means of communication improper.'

De László was asked when he ceased sending remittance abroad, the answer being 2 June 1916, and he explained that it was because his brother-in-law had warned him that he should not be sending money out of the country during wartime. This, he said, was the first warning he had received. He denied that he had stopped sending it because Madame van Riemsdyk had warned him that things were becoming 'rather complicated', and had asked him to send it via Blydensteins; in fact he did send one remittance that way before stopping of his own accord. He hadn't understood what she meant by becoming 'rather complicated', and had made up his mind on his own following his brother-in-law's advice. When Baron Mayendorff had mentioned his family during a sitting and asked whether there was anything he could do to help, De László had explained that no money could leave the country and Mayendorff himself had offered to take a cheque he would pay into a British account he held and then transmit the amount from an account abroad. It was on receipt of a letter from his brother, complaining that the money had never arrived, that he had had a visit from the Metropolitan Police warning him about it. Six months later he had received another warning from the director of public prosecutions.

After a brief reference to the Horn incident, the attorney general turned to what had been said to Basil Thomson about the letters to Hungary. Though the interview transcript said that he had only written to 'my own people', De László (who denied saying it) admitted he had also written to Baron Forster and sent a greeting to the bishop, and had forwarded a letter via Italy (which he had not mentioned in the interview when asked). He admitted having given a letter to Mayendorff to give to his wife to forward to Hungary from Switzerland, prompting the question, 'Does it occur to you that you have shown no little persistence, ingenuity, and resource in making and receiving communications with Hungary throughout the war?' He admitted that he knew now that it was wrong and regretted it very much; all his letters had been in good faith and he had not written anything about the war or mentioned anything that was not about family matters. His conscience was clear.

Re-examination by Sir John Simon began with a simple question: 'In whatever you have done, have you acted honestly?' to which the answer came, 'Honestly.' Regarding the reason given for the naturalisation, Soapy Simon pointed out that the form of words used was actually a direct copy of the guide for completion and suggested that the form had simply been filled in by the solicitor's clerk as a standard piece of work.

He then turned to the letter in *The Star*, reproduced in November 1914, pointing out that Arthur Balfour was not a lord (he wasn't ennobled until 1922) and that Guinness was not a member of Parliament. He also read out speeches that had been made in parliament by Asquith and Bonar Law, at about the date the letter was written, which praised Austria-Hungary and the emperor himself. The sentiment about Serbia, he said, was actually in keeping with the patriotic mood in Britain at the time. The letter was clearly an extract from a much longer one and, it was pointed out, De László's German was not good (an expert had looked over some of his correspondence and pointed out that he did not know the spelling of common words and his sentence construction was peculiar). The implication was that the translation was, at best, highly debateable.

Mention was made of a conversation De László had had with an expert in international law in 1912 about the process of getting naturalised and of an article in *Pall Mall* in which his intention of making England his home was quite clearly spelt out. Quotes were given from a letter from his sister, written in 1915, in which she said she had found three old letters from before the war in which he had told the family 'of being an Englishman'. De László agreed he had expressed this desire to a number of people, both British and Hungarian, long before the war 'or rumour of war was ever heard of'.

Sir John then mentioned various items of correspondence which he would like to have seen in court but which, unfortunately, were among those that had gone missing. Thomson had said he had sent the papers to MI5 and it had sent them either to the Treasury Solicitor or the Home Office, but now they couldn't be found. The 'precious postcard to your wife's maid with the alarming letter "L" on it', upon which De László had been questioned and had been unable to identify "L", was dismissed, as De László said he was not in the habit of reading servants' mail.

As it was getting late and Sir John hoped to interview Mrs De László it was decided to adjourn for the day.

Day Five

Lucy De László gave evidence that their children had all been brought up to be loyal to the British Crown and no other country. She said her husband had discussed naturalisation before 1914, and it had been her idea to correspond with his family through a neutral country. She confirmed her husband's evidence that she had written twice to Madame van Riemsdyk asking her to stop using the diplomatic bag for correspondence once she had discovered, from Mr Wyatt Williams, that it was an incorrect thing to do. The first letter had apparently not been received, so she had written again. She had written because her husband's grasp of German was peculiar. On being cross-examined she admitted that in marrying she had lost her nationality. She said her husband had decided to become British when he was ennobled by the Austrian emperor in 1912, but had thought that there was no reason to rush. It was only when their son was approaching 14, the age that would give Austria-Hungary a future claim on him for military service, that he decided to proceed. She said that the loss of British nationality would be a terrible disaster. She was unable to explain why Madame van Riemsdyk's daughter had written to her on 25 March 1915 saying that her mother would see her brother about forwarding letters. The suggestion about the future use of the diplomatic bag had been made by Madame van Riemsdyk and had been used since February that year.

Other witnesses spoke up for De László. Lord Lee said he was 'a person of great and at times embarrassing candour and of great honesty, and he was incapable of treacherous conduct'. He said he had first arranged to become a sponsor for the naturalisation in April 1914 and had urged De László to press on with it in July as he was ill and might not be able to help him in future. Sir John Lavery, the artist, testified that as far as he knew, no other artist had done as much for charity during the war and that he had a high opinion of De László's character and good faith. Mr John Hassall, who ran an art school in Earls Court, described him as a man of the highest honesty who wouldn't hurt a living animal, and his sons as model British boys. Mrs Margaret Warrender, who had known him since 1900, said she had spoken to him about naturalisation before 1912. She said that, even though De László knew she had brothers in high public service, he had never asked her for information. Colonel Repington, former military correspondent of *The Times*, said the same. After three more witnesses gave similar evidence, the chairman said it was unnecessary to call any more character witnesses.

After two more minor witnesses gave evidence and the two sides summarised their cases, the committee retired to consider. It was 3.37 p.m. They returned at 3.52 p.m. Their deliberations had taken fifteen minutes, less than that if you assume a couple of minutes at either end simply to get to and from the room in which they made them.

Mr Justice Salter then gave a long statement regarding whether it was necessary in the public interest to revoke De László's Certificate of Naturalisation. No man, he said, could give up his nationality of origin without severe mental conflict, so that was the letter to his brother dismissed. The sending of money to assist his family did not, in the circumstances, show that De László was disaffected or disloyal. The committee was satisfied that the sending of correspondence through the Dutch bag was only for safety and rapidity of transit, and that it was 'impossible to imagine anything more innocent'. When it came to the Horn incident, it was clearly a breach of the law and a

serious one. When it came to De László's behaviour, 'No justification can be found for his behaviour, but it is not difficult to
find a certain amount of excuse.' He had been taken unawares
and 'he had not sufficient decision to do the right thing at that
time', but, after consideration, he had gone to the police and it
was through him that Horn had been arrested. When it came to
deciding if his behaviour showed that he was disloyal or disaffected with the country or the king, it depended on whether he
had acted as he did because Horn was an enemy of the country
or whether he intended Horn should escape to join the Austrian
army. The committee had decided that 'his conduct was not
actuated by any hostility to this country or in favour of enemies
of this country ... but solely because he was a fugitive in distress
who threw himself upon his mercy and hospitality'.

The Winthrop Bowen incident was dismissed because the
committee decided that he had offered to send letters for De
László, but that De László had neither asked him to do so nor
taken up the offer. The author's reading of, 'Yes. By all means
send me any letters you wish me to forward' is that this is a
response to a request, not an offer conjured out of thin air, but
it is, I suppose, debateable.

The general tenor of all the correspondence examined, both
to and from his relatives, was purely of a family nature and neither side expressed any disloyalty to its side nor any hostility to
the other (though it was pointed out that the Austrian censor
would not allow such material through anyway).

Lastly:

> Mr László has been vouched as an honourable man and a loyal
> man by a considerable body of respectable witnesses, nearly all
> of whom have had good opportunity of forming an opinion,
> and several of whom, at any rate, are people who would not be
> likely to be easily deceived.

The various matters on which De László had been brought before the committee were gone over again, before, with some comments about the efficiency of the authorities in identifying a possibly serious matter during the course of the war and acting upon it, Mr Justice Salter concluded:

> We have enquired into this matter at considerable length. We have had every possible material and every possible assistance from Counsel on both sides, and we are satisfied that we have probed this matter to the bottom. We find it to be free from difficulty, and we have arrived at the conclusion, first, as I have already said, that no disloyalty or disaffection has been proved; next, that although there have been breaches of the law in regard to the money, and the carriage of letters, they were inadvertent and stopped when discovered; and with regard to the Horn incident, and to the case generally, we are satisfied that there has not been on the part of Mr László any conduct which would merit or justify the withdrawal from him of the British citizenship which he enjoys.

De László was cleared on all counts, after less than fifteen minutes' deliberation.

De László: Preferential Treatment

It's worth comparing the result of De László's hearing with that of Caroline Hanemann. There was no question raised at her hearing of her having broken any laws or regulations. There had been rumours about her but they had been investigated by MI5 and found to be unproven. She had written to her family in Germany during the war but her letters had all gone through Thomas Cook, the recognised intermediary. She had done her

bit in a small way for the war by making things for distressed
folk and soldiers, but obviously hadn't had the kind of money
that would have allowed her to make substantial investments
in war bonds. In her own way she had produced good men and
women to testify for her in her naturalisation – local worthies
and officials – and her mistress's doctor had written to the
committee commending her for the medical help she gave her.
Her reason for not naturalising earlier was simply because she
had never considered the possibility of war. She was stripped of
her British nationality.

De László had broken the rules on trading with the enemy;
he clearly knew more about the censorship rules than he admitted and went out of his way to avoid them. He had, whatever
he said, given aid to an escaped prisoner of war in the form of
money and had taken over twenty-four hours to report it to the
police, which would have given Horn plenty of time to escape
had he thought about it. De László, too, had been investigated
by MI5 and, though it was unable to prove anything in a court
of law, it had certainly had good reason to suspect him. It had
taken the committee two-and-a-half months to let Caroline
know that she was to be stripped of her naturalisation. It took
less than fifteen minutes to decide that De László was not to
be, and to tell him as much. It couldn't even be argued that the
armistice had taken place in the meantime; Caroline's interview
had been before the armistice but the decision was clearly taken
afterwards. In both cases the country was still technically at war.

If the Hanemann verdict was fair, then the De László verdict
was a disgrace, and vice versa.

Despite the result, MI5 was clearly not ashamed of the case.
On 28 June 1919 (the day after the hearing concluded), Major
Anson wrote a paragraph for the Report on Cable Censorship
in which he said:

A good instance of the value of Cable Censorship from our point of view, even when there is no ultimate conviction for espionage, is the well-known case of Philip de László. In this case our attention was first drawn to László by a suspicious telegram to Holland in February 1915, submitted by your section.

De László – John Bull

There was, the press reported, an excited buzz of conversation around the court following the verdict, and members of the audience pressed their congratulations upon De László and his wife. Most of the papers reported the matter in a straightforward manner, but there were popular periodicals that turned on him with a vengeance. Right-wing MP Horatio Bottomley, editor of *John Bull*, returned to the attack. An article headed 'The Peace That Passeth Understanding – Whitewashing De László' launched a scathing blast, accusing the people in high places of scurrying to defend one of their own. He quite flatly stated, 'László played the traitor, defied the laws made to safeguard and protect us in the war with the despicable Hun', and, 'The verdict of the Naturalisation (Revocation) Committee is a scandalous miscarriage of justice.'

The article went on to remind readers that De László had not been interned in a hurry, that he had been committing his offences for months before the police took action, that the committee had considered his case over many days, that the home secretary had confirmed the internment, and that a subsequent review in December 1917 had continued to keep De László a prisoner.

Bottomley pointed out that De László was 'rich, with influential friends', and lamented the appearance of one member of the government (the attorney general) eloquently setting out his offences while another, the chancellor of the exchequer, stood in the witness box 'with his hand on his heart, if not tears in his eyes, proclaiming his integrity and honour'. He questioned why Mrs Max Muller had not been called to give her evidence, the same point applying to Mr Henry Vincent Higgins MVO who had also promised to reveal conversations he had had with De László. He demanded an explanation from the attorney general. He also berated Sir John Simon for describing De László 'as one of the greatest artists the world has ever seen', and the director of public prosecutions who 'thought it consistent with his position and duty to the state to declare that De László had erred from "noble motives"'.

He further pointed out that 'if any poor German had done what rich De László did, there would be little of this slobbery sentiment forthcoming'. He sneered at these supposedly noble motives that had sent money for 'comforting the enemy'. He attacked the whole process, and the article concluded:

When he was cajoling votes last December, the Prime Minister promised that every interned Hun would be kicked out of the country and no enemies be allowed to enter it again. What value is to be attached to such a promise after this farce? Mr Justice Salter, Lord Hambledon and Judge Radcliffe, sitting in the High Court, in all the dignity of lounge suits, counsel making a pretence of judicial proceedings by wearing their wigs, the jury-box packed with society women, and no evidence taken on oath! I wonder how many British readers who followed the case have realised there was nothing really judicial about the enquiry. The whole thing was a sorry farce and the result is that a man who so offended against the law in the agonising years of war that he was interned, has now been confirmed in his British citizenship. László was anxious to make the best of both worlds. He succoured an Austrian escaped from Donington Hall, and postponed denouncing him to the police, fearing what would be said in Hungary. And he actually delayed becoming a British citizen out of regard for that old reprobate, the late Austrian Emperor, who ennobled him only two years before the war. He defied 'Dora' which every decent Britisher had to respect; he attempted to communicate with the enemy through five countries – Spain, Holland, Switzerland, Italy, America; he violated a diplomatic postbag; he sent expressions of sympathy to the enemy. And yet today, after this solemn farce of a pseudo trial, the claim of the State that the continuance of his naturalisation 'is not conducive to the public good' is denied; and the man who for our safety was sent to Brixton Prison, is to share with you and me – with every loyal and patriotic subject of the King, the priceless boon of British citizenship. László knows in which country his bread is buttered. If we lost the war he might have found refuge in his native land – where, according to the Attorney General 'his affections and sympathies are' – and have renounced the British naturalisation which cost him 'a severe mental conflict'. But a farcical Court has declared him to be truly British. And now, if he chooses, he can bring an action against me for calling him a traitor! But then the jury box would contain twelve honest men who love their country and honour their King, and who would not be influenced by any considerations of sycophancy and toadyism towards a social upstart, however well placed he might be with those of high estate.

De László's biography by Rutter claims that he made strenuous attempts to persuade his legal advisers to bring an action against Bottomley who, it has to be said, regardless of any rights or wrongs in this case, was a loathsome specimen who pandered to the most basic instincts of the electorate and was later found guilty of fraud. Wisely, De László said, they persuaded him against it, as it would simply bring the case back to public attention. Of course it could have meant that people such as Basil

Thomson, who had seen all the evidence, might have been put on oath and asked about it – and there would have been a jury. Given the result of the previous year's Pemberton Billing trial, it seems a wise decision.

There were others who wouldn't let it lie. On 29 July, in the House of Commons, the Liberal MP for East Edinburgh James Hogge asked the home secretary whether the charges against De László at the hearing before the Naturalisation Certificate Revocation Committee were the same that were brought before the committee appointed to deal with cases arising out of Order 14b of the Defence of the Realm Act, presided over by Mr Justice Sankey, or whether other allegations in addition were made by the Crown against Mr De László when his case was considered by Mr Justice Sankey's Committee. If the latter, would he state what those allegations were and why the case against Mr De László was not presented in the same manner to both committees?

Mr Shortt, the home secretary, replied:

As explained at the conclusion of the de László case by Mr. Justice Salter, the questions with which the Committee over which he presided had to deal were entirely different from those dealt with by the Committee presided over by Mr. Justice Sankey. The case, therefore, against Mr. de László did not assume precisely the same form before the two Committees. The Reports of Mr. Justice Sankey's Committee on the evidence and proceedings before them were laid before the Committee presided over by Mr. Justice Salter. The findings of Mr. Justice Salter's Committee as to the revocation of the certificate of naturalisation in no way conflict with the advice as to internment tendered by the Committee presided over by Mr. Justice Sankey.

Mr Hogge pressed his point, asking, 'If Mr. de László was acquitted by one committee as being practically guiltless, and therefore

eligible for British citizenship, why was he interned by the other?'
To which Mr Shortt replied:

> Because the two questions are totally different. In the case of
> internment it is a question whether it is necessary on any ground
> of suspicion for the safety of the country. You can run no risks.
> In the other you go into the whole of the facts and thrash them out.

In fact this wasn't quite an honest and complete answer.
Mr Hogge had specifically asked whether other allegations had
been made and 'whether he would state what those allegations
were and why the case against Mr. de László was not presented
in the same manner to both Committees?'

A memo in the Home Office file discusses the question while
preparing the Home Secretary's answer and notes that it is
almost certainly based on the questions asked in the *John Bull*
article about whether vital evidence had been suppressed. Some
evidence presented to the first committee had indeed not been
presented to the second. Four people who had given evidence
the first time had not done so on the second occasion – partly
because one was dead and another unavailable, while the attorney general, it was claimed, thought the other two weren't worth
using. But other evidence was not presented to the hearing,
or at least to the public part of it. The secret service reports were
by 'general agreement in which the Attorney General agreed',
not used because they 'could not properly be used'. The reports
of the original Sankey Committee, which did discuss the secret
service reports in some detail, was put before the second committee 'who could, if they had thought proper, [have] pursued
the matter further'. But the allegations were never put forward
to the second committee in public, and the home secretary and
the attorney general never mentioned that allegations had been
made that De László was a spy.

Did the British Always Get It Right?

MI5 was certainly pleased with itself at the end of the war. The home secretary (without naming the organisation) had told Parliament that the German spy organisation in Britain had been smashed in August 1914 and never recovered. A dozen spies had been caught and executed and many more imprisoned, usually because they were neutrals employed by the Germans and it made more sense to show clemency where neutral governments were involved. A worldwide security organisation based on the restriction of travel visas to suspicious foreigners, run abroad by SIS but coordinated by MI5 in London, made travel by potential foreign agents prohibitive, and an aggressive policy of running double agents abroad, again co-ordinated by MI5, had attacked German espionage in its stations in Holland, Switzerland and the United States. But were the British authorities always right?

Not always, and their pursuit of some suspected agents could be both blinkered and cruel. One such, though his main persecutors were Basil Thomson and Special Branch, was Baron Louis von Horst, a German businessman with extensive interests in the international hop trade, particularly between the USA and Britain. Louis von Horst was born in Germany in 1865, but moved to the USA as a child and was later naturalised there. Together with his brothers he established a company that purchased Californian hops direct from the farmers and sold them to east coast brewers, cutting out the old middle men brokers to the advantage of both sides. They went international and by purchasing hops in this way, and expanding into hop growing themselves, the brothers were able to undercut British hop producers with their imports. Louis ran the British side of their business. Though accused of 'dumping' and selling inferior hops by the British growers, and subject to a hostile press, the Horst brothers prospered in the years leading up to the First World War. Unfortunately, Louis had a fatal weakness, though he can hardly have foreseen it as such. During a period of great financial and personal trouble following the 1906 San Francisco earthquake, which had destroyed his hop harvest, he had become close to, and dependent for a short time on, a wealthy, twenty years younger, Irish-American woman journalist named Lilian Scott Troy, who was also a political radical.

Under her influence he too began to mix in radical circles and when, during the 1912 Dock Strike, Lilian overcommitted herself in supporting food kitchens for the relief of strikers' families, he quite happily paid to provide 100,000 meals. Troy also talked him into supporting the *Daily Herald*, the new national Labour newspaper, and it was her influence that made him take an interest in both the Suffragette movement and in Irish nationalism. The latter interest was, in part, motivated by the hope of establishing hop farms in Ireland, but it meant meetings with Irish politicians, including Roger Casement, and that some comments he made quite innocently about German shipping visiting Irish ports were later taken wildly out of context.

On the outbreak of war, von Horst was invited by the US consul general to assist those Germans who were still in Britain, some 8,000 of whom, having lost their jobs, were on the verge of destitution. Known as the 'Emergency Committee for the Assistance of Germans, Austrians and Hungarians in Distress', and funded to a large extent by money collected in America by Troy, the committee came under attack from a hostile press and, after one committee meeting, von Horst was arrested and taken to Scotland Yard. Here he was questioned by Thomson and only released on the intervention of assistant police commissioner F.T. Bigham (brother of Charles Clive Bigham). But Thomson had him in his sights, and when he applied for permission to leave the country it was refused on the grounds that he was German; his explanation that he had never sworn an oath to Germany, had voted in US elections and that his German title was a purely honorary one (awarded for sponsorship of a German opera school) was not accepted and he was compelled to register as an enemy alien, which he did on the last day of the deadline.

Special Branch produced a report in which they acknowledged that a Briton who had attached himself to the Suffragette movement, socialism and Irish nationalism 'might have been ascribed to a restless sympathy to all who believe themselves to be oppressed' but that, as a German, 'one can come to no other conclusion but that he is a German agent of a very dangerous type'. Horst was arrested at the end of August 1914 and spent the war in internment before being expelled in 1919, his businesses in Britain having collapsed in the interim.

The truth of the story is that von Horst was enamoured of the much younger Lilian Troy and went out of his way to help and support her. She was absolutely an American and, therefore, pretty much untouchable without rock solid evidence, but the authorities were able to create just enough fog around von Horst's nationality to allow them to get at her through him. Their relationship was known about (she is referred to as his 'paramour'), but ignored as a factor. Though it was a Special Branch case, MI5 did, in a report from March 1917, describe him as 'a most dangerous German agent'.

Even after the war, when von Horst made genuine attempts to restart his hop business in Ireland, he was obstructed at all points by the British authorities.

It's clear, from this one example, that the British authorities were not infallible and could be vindictive. But was the Internment Committee correct when it agreed to keep De László interned? The short and simple answer has to be yes. The review committee, much as it didn't like it, said so. Sir John Simon, and through him De László (no doubt through gritted teeth), admitted this during the Denaturalisation Committee. MI5, through Vernon Kell, admitted it was a difficult case (possibly because of his prominent connections – in 1917 it formed a special sub-section, G3 (ii), for investigation into suspected persons in diplomatic, financial and political circles), but was quite satisfied that it had done a good job in getting him detained.

De László the Spy

The Denaturalisation Committee wasn't something MI5 wanted, nor had its investigations been made with it in mind. In fact, MI5 investigations were made with the intention of preventing espionage, which did not necessarily mean arresting and prosecuting spies or even having them interned. There were a number of cases where potential enemy agents were identified before they travelled to Britain and it was simple enough to refuse them visas to travel – this was probably the most effective means of preventing spying and, in 1915, German agents were already reporting that travel restrictions were making their job harder and they were having difficulty getting into the country. Agents could also be 'turned' into working for MI5 while appearing still to work for the enemy. Such 'double agents' were given much more prominence in the public eye after the Second World War, when the whole network of carefully controlled XX (Double Cross) agents was gradually revealed. In fact double agents were common in the First World War too. The American agent codenamed COMO has already been mentioned, but there were many others. One was a former Swiss army officer, naturalised as British, who was persuaded by military intelligence in France to contact German intelligence in Switzerland who recruited him as a spy and sent him back to London. Here he gave MI5 'considerable valuable information about German methods, identity of their chief agents and so forth and has also worked very satisfactorily in maintaining spy correspondence, under our instructions, with the German Secret Service'. After some deliberation he was allowed to become an MI5 officer once the particular double game he was involved in came to a natural conclusion. Double agents operated in the Far East and Mexico, and there is even some slight evidence that MI5 was involved in faking an explosion at a munitions factory to support the work of a double agent in Britain in 1918. From MI5's perspective, a dangerous enemy agent had been effectively neutralised. If conclusive evidence had been obtained then De László could have been turned or, as was more usual, passed to Special Branch for arrest and prosecution.

Before the denaturalisation hearing, the authorities carried out, as best they could, an examination of the French Secret Service documents. They were acknowledged as being the most important evidence, but also that it was doubtful how far they could be used. They began with the first note, dated 7 July, noting that:

> László has access to splendid political information.
> László did not deny all knowledge of 'Madame G', but merely said he could not remember who it was.
> The Dutch Diplomatic Bag was used by De László.

Of the letter dated 12 July they commented:

> By this time the French Secret Service have got hold of De László's name.
>
> The mechanism of the passing of the secret information is quite correct, viz László has access to Official Circles, he was in touch with a Dutch subject, and the Dutch Subject was in touch with Austria, and very probably by Switzerland, see as to this László's statement to Scotland Yard.

The letter dated 24 July prompted:

> The French Secret Service have found out that the intermediary
> is known as the 'ami Hollondaise'.

Of the letter dated 14 June, that had been procured by
Thomson's agent, they were effusive:

> This document is addressed to László at his correct address. Let
> us assume that the superscription is a forgery. The contents of
> the letter, however, are too strong to be disregarded.
>   László did wish to recover his nationality.
>   He had access to Society, Court and Intellectual circles.
>   He was a vain man; hence his correspondent flatters him.
>   'Madame G' reappears. This is a remarkable coincidence.
>   Enclosure
>   The 'ami Hollondaise' reappears; again a curious coincidence.
>   The information alleged to have been furnished by László was
> easily within his power, having regard to his position.
>   The nationality question crops up again.
>   The last paragraph is true, but hardly the thing which Laszlo
> would advertise.
>   Two further points should be noted.
>   Madame van Riemsdyk was reported to MI5 by their
> Rotterdam agent, on August 4th last, as a person known to have
> acted as intermediary for correspondence with Austria.
>   The Comte de Soissons, writing to Basil Thomson on
> September 24th last, says 'HE IS CERTAINLY UNFRIENDLY
> TO US, IF NOT DELIBERATELY AND MALICIOUSLY
> DANGEROUS'. Thomson does not think much of the Comte's
> judgment, but this is certainly strong language.

So the authorities felt that the information was internally consistent and matched other information they knew (the use of the bag) that very few others did. It might be argued that MI5 somehow forged the correspondence, but there are letters on the file from Bigham, who worked for SIS, and it would have been remarkably foolish to involve a member of another agency, whose job it was to liaise closely with the French, in an act of forgery. It would also be incredibly risky to plant a story claiming that the king was having doubts about the war. It could be argued that the French wrote the notes as a means of discrediting De László in the eyes of their allies, but what purpose would that serve? A more interesting theory might be that the documents were created by the Austrian secret service and planted on the French in order to cause problems for a man they considered a traitor and renegade. This is plausible apart from the fact that they would be using a double agent who could be better deployed in planting false military or political information that could be used to win the war.

So if De László was a spy, why wasn't MI5 able to prove it? There would have been immediate problems with MI5's investigation. It was clear from the correspondence (the letter dated 16 July) that Madame G and De László had already felt watched and had been warned to keep their heads down. Any evidence would surely have been destroyed once they thought they were watched. Provided De László had sent his reports by hand to Madame G (whoever she was), they wouldn't have been picked up by the special supervision exercised over his correspondence. We know, from his own admission, that letters destined for transmission in the bag were taken by hand, usually by Miss Lundquist, and there is only his word as to how many she said she actually took. As a Dutch subject, Madame G would have had every excuse to visit the legation; it's also possible the Dutch had reasons of their own for helping them out.

Adrienne Van Reimsdyk was sister of the Dutch foreign minister and it's interesting to ponder whether the Dutch might
have been getting something out of transmitting (and reading)
the messages De László was alleged to have sent. Holland was
caught between a rock and a hard place. It was heavily dependent upon imports, which were strictly controlled by the British
in order to prevent re-export to Germany (SIS obtained copies
of customs manifests for legitimate exports, which were analysed closely for any sign of Holland breaking her re-export
agreements), and yet bounded along most of her frontier by
a Germany that had a much larger army and upon which the
Dutch were heavily dependent for coal supplies. Maintaining
neutrality was difficult and, though Dutch financial institutions and merchants made substantial profits from dealings
with both sides, conditions in the country were deteriorating.
The British blockade had caused food shortages leading to food
riots; fears that Germany would use the winter of 1916–17 to
bully Holland by restricting coal supplies had not come to pass,
but it remained a distinct possibility as relations between the
two countries deteriorated during 1917 as the effects of the
German submarine blockade also began to bite.

In April 1917, British double agent COMO reported a meeting he had had with a member of the German general staff who
had warned him that there would be war with Holland within a
fortnight. There was little doubt that the German army would
sweep through the country rapidly. It was important, then, that
the Dutch government kept closely in touch with developments and opinions abroad. The admission by a Dutch consul
in 1918 that the Dutch Foreign Ministry contained a division
'for facilitating private communication between people residing in belligerent countries' suggests that there was a deliberate
policy of encouraging private contacts, possibly with the same
aim as the British censorship – to use it as a means of gathering

intelligence from abroad. De László's communications and the alleged reports might have proved invaluable to them. It is unlikely we'll ever know – Dutch intelligence burned their files when Germany did finally invade, in May 1940.

De László, again by his numerous admissions, felt close to his former homeland and deeply regretted its treatment of him as a result of his naturalisation. He felt closer still to his family who remained there. Whether or not he wanted the return of his nationality, he had strong motives for wishing to help his old country. He had splendid opportunity to do so. He was close to the circles that ran the war and to the diplomats in London who could supply, unknowingly, high-level information. Evidence was given that he asked questions about supplies and consumption of ammunition. The alleged means of transmitting the information matched a route that De László was known to use, the Dutch diplomatic bag, and it's interesting that he only ever sent his personal mail to the legation by hand (meaning a forty-minute walk from his house in Palace Gate to the Dutch Legation in Montagu Place), which conveniently meant it never entered the postal system. MI5 doesn't seem to have been aware of any propaganda role for him before the French told it, but then discovered that he had talked pointedly to his clients about Britain's allies, denigrating the Russians and claiming that America's entry into the war was simply to create a military spirit in preparation for her own war with Japan and Mexico. He had contact addresses for known and suspected pacifists and pacifist propagandists such as Szebenyei, who was interned for a likely connection to Hungarian propaganda; Robert Dell, the Fabian pacifist; Rudolph Said-Ruete, who wrote pro-German booklets; and Countess Helena Pourtales, who supplied English-language German newspapers to America. He had copies of propaganda leaflets and books.

Though he claimed ignorance of the censorship and 'Trading with the Enemy' rules he was remarkably adept at getting round

them, and despite many of the people 'in the know', such as the
Board of Trade employees, thinking he should be prosecuted for
his breaches of the regulations, he wasn't. Lots of people, who
had committed much more trivial breaches of the same rules,
were. Everyone was aware of his connections (he was an invet-
erate name dropper) and his society friends rallied round to
support one of their own. It's hard to avoid the conclusion that
it was considered not to be in the public interest to denatural-
ise him because it would undermine the positions of his many
friends in the Lords and Commons (including a former prime
minister and a serving chancellor).

Kind and loving family man though he undoubtedly was,
Philip De László had a strong streak of self-interest running
through him. Caught in a difficult situation not of his own
making, he tried to play both ends against the middle, toadying to
the British establishment and providing help to the Hungarians
in the form of propaganda and information. Whichever side lost,
he was going to be able to claim he was on the other.

The Spy who Painted the Queen

W ITH HIS CHARACTER apparently vindicated by the committee, De László was free to go back to his profession, and he completed twenty portraits by the end of 1919, earning £8,000. He resumed advertising in *The Times* and in 1920 completed forty-two portraits, earning over £20,000. Prominent sitters gradually flocked to him again and he painted, among many others, US President Harding, Benito Mussolini and Queen Marie of Roumania.

In early 1925 the Home Office received an enquiry from the Lord Chamberlain asking whether De László was suitable to be received at Court. A two-page memorandum was drawn up which set out the basics of the events that had led up to his internment and the appearance before the Revocation Committee. It concluded:

> The Committee found that the continuance of his naturalization certificate was not inconsistent with public good and reported that its revocation was not desirable. After these findings the internment order against László was revoked by the Home Secretary Mr Shortt in July 1919.

Mr De László is therefore now a British subject and is entitled
to all political and other rights, powers and privileges to which
a natural born British subject is entitled. Under Article 213 of
the Treaty of Trianon Hungary recognised any new nationality
acquired by her nationals under the laws of the Allied Powers,
and it is clear that Hungary has no longer any claim in regard to
Mr De László.

There would seem to be no reason now, so far as the Home
Office point of view is concerned, why Mr De László should
not be received at Court. He is of course a well-known person
socially and is I believe an intimate friend of Mr Austen
Chamberlain, who has known him for a good many years.

The memo is initialled by 'H R D' and dated 9/2/25. Another
official has hand written beneath, 'I have written to the Lord
Chamberlain accordingly.'

Shortly after this enquiry he had painted Rosemary,
the daughter of Lord Cromer, the Lord Chamberlain, and had
received a letter of gratitude and appreciation from Lady Cromer.
He painted Lady Cromer herself a few weeks later and there followed, shortly afterwards, an invitation to a Buckingham Palace
garden party, which delighted De László, who had not been
invited to a Court function since his release from internment.
Here he was presented to the king by Lord Cromer himself.

The return to Court circles removed any potential problems
from De László painting members of the Royal Family, and in
1931 he painted the Duke and Duchess of York (later, of course,
to become King George VI and Queen Elizabeth, the Queen
Mother). Further contact with the family led to him painting the
7-year-old Princess Elizabeth, already heir to the throne, in 1933.
The finished piece went on display at Knoedlers of Bond Street
that June, and reproductions in black and white and in colour
proved very popular. The *Illustrated London News* ran a full-page

image of the portrait in its issue of 30 December 1933, describing it as 'charming'. It is a nice portrait. Of Princess Elizabeth, De László was quoted as saying, 'She is the most amazing child I have ever painted – I have never met such an intelligent child. She talks as easily and as wisely as a grown-up.'

He continued to paint and to travel, visiting the USA, Spain, Morocco, France and Italy, and was fêted on a visit to Hungary in 1935. He continued to work hard and painted the Archbishop of York, the Duke of Kent and, in 1936, the mistress of the King of Roumania.

De László died, following a heart attack and after a long and slow descent into ill-health, on 22 November 1937. His memorial service at St Margaret's, Westminster, was attended by a host of society names – though, perhaps surprisingly, few of the really highest in the land. His friend and witness Austen Chamberlain had died earlier in the year. The Archbishop of Canterbury, Cosmo Lang, gave the blessing. *The Times* obituary described him as 'the most fashionable portrait painter of modern times', but appeared to imply that part of his success was due to his ability to flatter his sitters. Of his artistic style, the obituarist said:

> His work was large and broad in style but lacked subtlety, both as regards characterization and form and colour, and for all his command of the picture space he was weak in construction. He succeeded by his power of generalizing a conception of the sitter which was both complimentary to the individual and suggestive of the environment.

His estate, on death, was valued at £141,000 gross – the equivalent of almost £9,000,000 today.

APPENDIX 1

THE ONE-ARMED MAN

I N MAY 1933 De László wrote to his friend István Bárczy, permanent under-secretary in the Hungarian prime minister's
office, regarding a court case pending against him in Paris
brought by one Frederic Decseny. He wrote:

> [Decseny] is a miserable specimen of humanity who tried to
> blackmail me. I have never seen or heard of him … Now that
> he cannot get money out of me, he continues to be unpleasant.
> You can imagine what it means to me to be dragged through the
> French newspapers associated with such a scoundrel.

De László's French lawyer was looking for some official
Hungarian documentation confirming the reason Decseny
had been imprisoned, and De László asked Bárczy for help in
obtaining it. Whether he did or not is unknown, but De László
definitely thanked him for his efforts and, as his biographer says,
'the matter was definitely closed on 2 June 1933'.

On 22 April 1933 the *Daily Mail* had run a short story
headed, 'Mr P A De László – Lawsuit sequel to spy case'. It read:

Mr P A de László the famous painter who lives in London, was sued yesterday for £36 compensation by Frederic Decseny, said to be a Hungarian, who alleged that he had been imprisoned for two years during the war as a British spy following his denunciation by Mr de László.

Decseny, a one-armed man, waved his remaining arm excitedly when the judge asked him his nationality. Dashing up to the Judge's dais, he shouted 'I am a man without a nationality.'

Mr de László's counsel, Maitre Yvonne Menjaud, a pretty woman, asked that the case be adjourned for a fortnight, to which the court agreed.

Frederic Decseny (sometimes spelt Decsenyi or Deczeny) had been born in Volocz, Hungary, in 1885, emigrated to the USA in 1902 and, having lost his arm in an accident while working for the Erie Railroad Company, took up work as a clerk in New York where he became naturalised on 1 June 1907. He had left the USA in 1909 and spent some time in England and then in Belgium and Hungary. He applied for an American passport at the United States consulate in Budapest on 25 August 1914 with the intention of returning to America within six months. As an American and therefore a neutral he was capable of travelling more or less freely around the continent and was even able to visit and leave Britain.

In 1924 he applied to the US consul at Coblenz for papers, asserting that he had been imprisoned in Germany during the First World War. As the *Daily Mail* report confirms, this, he asserted, was because De László had told the Hungarian authorities that he was a British spy.

Prior to the court case, it's known he had approached the British Embassy in Paris and been rebuffed, because he wrote to the Home Office complaining about its attitude to him. It, in turn, approached the Foreign Office seeking further information and specifically saying, in its request, that his visit to the embassy had been to 'give some information about Mr De László's activities during the war'and asking that the embassy provide more information about the allegations.

The Foreign Office, in answer to a Freedom of Information request, confirmed that its file (reference C 5659/3359/21) had been destroyed during its normal weeding process, but provided a copy of its file summary, which confirmed the story as given above. The Home Office file reference number on the summary proved to be De László's naturalisation file, which has clearly been weeded (section 113 was noted as 'Confidential – This sheet and the dummies for the subnos. to which it refers must not leave the registry' has been removed and the Home Office claim no record of it). The register of correspondence (HO 46/286) for 1933 confirms that a copy of the unspecified allegation against De László, which was received on 31 March from Decseny himself, was passed by the Home Office to MI5. It was also, presumably, passed to the Foreign Office for its comments on the allegations against the Paris Embassy. MI5 replied to the Home Office on 21 April, but the surviving note reads, 'Report unable to find any trace of a (the next word is unclear but seems to read) liaison.' Liaison presumably means meeting, so Decseny seems to be suggesting that, at some stage, he and De László had met.

If Decseny and De László had met (which De László categorically denied), when might it have been? In his interrogation of 15 August 1917, he did mention meeting an unnamed Hungarian in 1914. He said:

When the war broke out a Hungarian who I had never seen before came over to England because he thought it was the safest place for a Hungarian to be. He brought me a letter of recommendation from an old friend of mine. I was so pleased to learn from this letter that my mother was still alive that I gave him a letter to take back, which was, however taken away from him. He was the very man whom I invited to lunch with me. He went home and made a big story out of it. He asked me what my position was and I said 'I am a British subject.' (This was not then known in Hungary, it came out afterwards.) Then this man went back to Hungary and made a terrible row in the papers …

Later in the interview, De László said that his visitor was 'Sbenenyei' (presumably the journalist Szebenyei, Hungarian correspondent for the *Morning Post* whose name appeared in his address book), but in the second interview he said the man was 'Professor B', whose name he could not remember. It seems unlikely a Hungarian could have travelled freely between the two countries once they were at war. Britain had declared war on Austria-Hungary on 12 August 1914. De László's application for citizenship had not been made until 15 August and wasn't granted until the 29th. He didn't take the oath of allegiance until 2 September. Decseny was in Budapest on 25 August as he applied for an American passport at the US consulate there on that date. With such a passport (passports were rarely required before the outbreak of the war but rapidly became necessary), Decseny could travel across Europe, enter Britain and return. He certainly fancied himself as a journalist, describing himself in later life as a correspondent for both the London *Daily Mail* and the *Detroit Free Press*. He is surely the same person referred to in a letter from Adrienne van Riemsdyk dated 19 October 1914, which said, 'Your Hungarian friend has not been to see us so far – perhaps he went straight through to Pesht.'

If it was blackmail that Decseny was attempting, it seems curious that he had gone to the British Embassy with his allegations before launching his claim through the courts. The Foreign Office file summary sheets say that he had written complaining about his treatment there on 29 March. The sum of £36 (worth £2,250 today) seems trivial and more like a token sum designed to get the case into a court for publicity purposes.

The curious thing is that De László seemed to think that the story was well covered in the French press, but searches of the online versions of *Le Figaro*, *L'Echo de Paris*, *L'Humanité*, *Le Matin*, *L'Ouest-Éclair*, *Le Petit journal*, *Le Petit Parisien* and *Le Temps* make no mention of it. It doesn't even receive attention in an article in *Le Temps* of 2 May 1933 (while the trial was supposedly taking place), which mentions De László's art briefly in a general article.

Decseny knew something about De László's wartime activities – that seems clear. Unfortunately it has not (yet) proved possible to discover what it was.

MORE LINKS
TO ROYALTY

WITH DE LÁSZLÓ'S death, MI5 would normally have closed its file on him. It has not been released, despite files on other better-known suspects (W.H. Auden, Jacob Bronowski, J.B. Priestley and George Orwell among them) having been opened in recent years. It's possible that it has been destroyed as part of MI5's routine weeding and destruction policy, but another intriguing possibility remains.

John De László, Philip's fifth son, had an affair in the late 1940s with the wife of Group Captain Peter Townsend, the Battle of Britain hero and equerry to King George VI. The couple divorced in 1952 and John married her in 1953. The divorce hung over Group Captain Townsend and, in the atmosphere of the time, he was not allowed to remarry within the Church of England. When he and Princess Margaret fell in love and there was talk in the press of them marrying, the matter reached as high as the prime minister, Winston Churchill, then aged 79 and in his final term. The couple, who seem to have had a real and genuine affection for each other, were forced apart by the attitudes prevalent in the upper echelons of society at the time. The princess could not, quite simply, be allowed to get married outside the Church of England, and the Church of England was not going to change its view on remarrying a divorced man.

A few years ago I mentioned the De László case as part of a talk I was giving. At the end I was approached by a man I had known vaguely for many years who said that the name De László was one he had known well, but that he hadn't heard it in fifty years. As a young man he had worked as a telephone engineer and was based in south-east England. The new Mrs De László and her husband lived in his area at the end of a country lane and shared a party line with the other houses. This meant that a single line ran up the lane and every house had a telephone connected to it. One bill was issued for the whole line and, of course, only one telephone could be used at a time. According to my friend, this posed a problem for the other line users as Mrs De László spent hours on the phone and would only pay a set percentage of the bill rather than the amount equivalent to her usage. The other line users made repeated complaints to the GPO, who always replied that this was a matter the line users had to sort out between themselves. Eventually, however, the complaints became so persistent that my friend's boss sent him to examine the line to see if there was any way the De Lászlós' telephone could be connected separately. On opening the junction box at the end of the lane he was confronted by something that, while in training, he had once been shown and told, 'You will never see one of these but, if you do, you are to report its presence to your manager and immediately forget that you ever saw it.' His manager turned pale on being advised of this item, and repeated the advice that, as my friend had signed the Official Secrets Act, he was never to mention it. He hadn't mentioned it to a soul until we spoke about it over fifty years later. Though the exact nature of 'it' was not specified, I think we were both clear that 'it' was a tap on the telephone line – and the fact that he had been shown one and recognised it means it was an official one. As far as he knew, the problem with the party line was never resolved.

Whether it was an MI5 tap, or perhaps one from the police or another agency, we will probably never know – or, indeed, quite why the calls were being listened to. But someone official considered there was a good reason. Though Philip De László had been dead for twenty years, there may be cross references on his MI5 file that will reveal things that, even now, the powers that be do not want us to know.

DID THE FRENCH
REPORTS EVEN EXIST?

THERE'S AN INTERESTING question relating to the French secret service reports. Did they, in fact, exist or could they have been fabricated by MI5 itself on the basis of other, even more secret sources?

The biography of Sir Henry Curtis-Bennett, written by Roland Wild and Curtis-Bennett's son, tells how, concerned that plots were being fomented in Paris by the Russian intelligence service, an attempt was made to access documents being carried by a Russian official travelling from Paris to Russia via London and Scotland. It seems far-fetched: it involved the drugging of the Russian in Edinburgh and the rushing of his bag on an express train to London, where it was opened, the contents photographed and the whole bag (which had to be retied in exactly the same way) rushed back to Scotland before its carrier awoke. However, it's not utterly impossible. Almost exactly the same story is given in *Private and Official,* the biography of Sir Ronald Dockray Waterhouse, though in this case it names the head of the Russian intelligence service as Ignatieff. Waterhouse served as an MI5 officer between May 1915 and the end of April 1918 as head of the Military Permit Office in Bedford Square, which issued travel permits to the military zone in France between 1915 and October 1917, a job described as 'a very responsible position, as in addition to dealing with questions of permits to France for British subjects who are frequently of high rank, he has to maintain very close and cordial relations with the French passport office'. He left the Permit Office in October 1917 to become head of MI5 G3. Included amongst G3's duties were 'Special investigations into the cases of suspected persons in diplomatic, financial and political circles'. It's quite likely, then, that if investigations were being carried out into material passing through the country via the diplomatic bag, he would at least have been aware of it. The biography was written by his widow, Nourah Waterhouse, and in fact describes what appear to be two attempts to access diplomatic material, the other being an attempt to get into the Chinese bag.

Oddly enough, though it makes no mention of attempting to break into the bag, there's a file on Ignatieff in TNA, dated 29 November 1917, which describes worries about his contacts with the German secret service. There were actually two Ignatieff brothers: Alexis, the military attaché and Paul, head of the secret service in Paris. Paul had taken over in Paris in 1916 and, the French said, the information he had been providing to them had gone from excellent to bad, then, recently, to dangerous and probably false. The French had him and his agents followed and came to the conclusion that he was working with the new Bolshevik government in Russia and possibly co-operating with the Germans. The officer compiling the report, Major Claude Dansey, a former MI5 man now working for SIS, concluded, 'in order to guard our own interests we should not neglect the possibility that Ignatieff is willing to assist the Germans'. Given the facilities the British granted the Russians in terms of travel, a Foreign Office official commented, 'we agree that the matter is one of considerable importance and would be glad to consult the

French as to the expediency of allowing these Russian couriers the facilities they have hitherto enjoyed'. Since the Foreign Office had not been told officially about the matter, it specifically requested that Kell ask the director of military intelligence to raise the matter with them. Presumably the break into the bag happened after this.

The British had long been aware that companies, individuals and German officials had been using neutral countries' diplomatic bags or post as a means of avoiding the world-wide censorship system. Items of intercepted ordinary mail sometimes made reference to it. A letter from a German lady dated 29 July 1916, intercepted on the high seas, described how she received letters from the USA via the Colombian diplomatic bag between Washington and Berlin and through the Dutch Foreign Ministry. An intercepted telegram between Buenos Aires and Hamburg said the easiest way to get a letter through was via the Argentine legation. Two letters sent from Germany in the US diplomatic bag and posted on to Tonga in the ordinary mail were intercepted by the censor in Samoa and reported to London by the New Zealand government.

There is some evidence that diplomatic mail was being opened as early as 1915, as three packets addressed to the Swedish legation in Washington had been found to contain enclosures addressed to the German Embassy. A packet stamped by the Dutch Ministry of Foreign Affairs opened by the Singapore censor in June 1916 contained a packet from Vienna to the Dutch East Indies. A letter bearing a Peruvian legation seal, and stamped by it, was intercepted on the SS *Frederik VIII* and, on being opened, was found to contain pro-German propaganda destined for Venezuela. His Majesty's Minister in Bangkok informed the Foreign Office that he was suspicious that the Dutch Legation Bag was being used to carry official German correspondence to Java. It's clear that the ordinary censorship was no respecter of the stamps and seals of neutral consulates or embassies, though there is no mention of diplomatic bags, which appear to have been sacrosanct.

It's generally assumed that the opening of foreign diplomatic bags by the British secret services began in the 1920s when SIS established their N Section, probably a joint section with MI5, that was reputed to 'have a team of thirty seamstresses' who could open and re-sew a diplomatic bag 'in a fashion calculated to avoid detection'. As a natural sceptic, the current author doubted the validity of some of these stories until a former member of a foreign diplomatic service, who had sealed bags regularly, thought through the process and described how, theoretically, opening one undetected might be done. The method postulated matched, in the most important details, the method allegedly used by MI5 to open Ignatieff's courier's bag. It does seem possible that this might have occurred, but it would have involved a great deal of deception, particularly of the Foreign Office, which was notoriously sensitive to such matters and which, through its control of the Secret Service Fund, was to a large part MI5's paymasters.

One point militating strongly against the breaking into diplomatic bags is a paragraph in the Special Section report in KV 4/16 which says:

> Under the Defence of the Realm Regulations the only media for the conveyance of uncensored written or printed communications from this country to neutral countries was the Private bags despatched from the various Embassies in London. The Diplomatic objections to any interference with these bags have always been too strong to permit of steps being taken to examine their contents, even when there has been reason to suspect that their immunity was being taken advantage of by enemy agents and it has always been felt that this channel constituted a grave source of danger which it has not been possible to eliminate.

But they would say that, wouldn't they?

WHAT BECAME OF THE OTHERS?

Arpad Horn

The unfortunate Arpad Horn, following his arrest and questioning, was returned to Donington Hall and placed in solitary confinement, with only one hour's exercise each morning and evening, for forty-one days. On 29 August he was court-martialled and sentenced to fourteen days' imprisonment, for which he was transferred to Chelmsford Prison. Here, he complained, he was 'shut up in a narrow cell and was allowed to spend 1 hour morning and evening in the prison court yard under the supervision of 3 sentries. For exercise there was a space of about 15 x 4 metres where I was placed together with English convicts.' He wasn't allowed newspapers, his food was restricted and he was expected to pay for it, he was only allowed to smoke in the exercise yard and his cell was so damp he fell ill from the effects. After his sentence he was transferred to Dyffryn Aled, a POW camp in north Wales surrounded by moors and far from the coast. From here he raised complaints

about his treatment via the Swedish legation, which was looking after Austro-Hungarian interests in Britain for the duration
of the war. Presumably he was repatriated in 1919.

Adrienne van Riemsdyk

Adrienne van Riemsdyk's only daughter, Marguerite Louise,
married a British officer, Major Samuel John Barrington of
the Suffolk Regiment, on 24 May 1919. Curiously, one of the
witnesses was Colonel Oppenheim, British military attaché to
The Hague, who had had extremely close links to the British
secret services during the war. Adrienne van Riemsdyk herself
died, after a long illness, while visiting her daughter and son-in-
law in East Anglia, on 19 October 1919.

Vernon Kell and MI5

Despite enormous cuts in MI5's budget and staff numbers post-
war and its relegation to the monitoring of foreign spies and
communist agitation in the armed forces (communism generally – industrial relations, terrorism and sedition passed back
to Special Branch), Vernon Kell was regarded as a safe pair of
hands and steered the organisation through the difficult waters
of the 1920s. In part because MI5 was able to expose two communist 'moles' within Special Branch, and partly because of the
rise of Fascism in Italy and Germany, the organisation took on
increased responsibilities in the early 1930s, absorbing part of
The Branch, as well as a top secret organisation used by SIS to
carry out investigations within the UK (a breach of the rule that
it should only gather information abroad). The organisation
expanded in the late 1930s in anticipation of war with Germany,

but for all Kell's planning, MI5 came close to collapse once again when war broke out, under the sheer volume of enquiries. It had planned a huge round-up of potentially hostile aliens on the outbreak of war, but this had been severely watered down by the Home Office, only to emerge again with the crisis brought on by Dunkirk in 1940. In the resulting chaos, Kell was obliged by Churchill himself to take retirement, with his deputy, Eric Holt Wilson, joining him. Despite threats of mass resignations among the MI5 staff (which didn't occur), the organisation soldiered on to become, once again, a highly efficient counter-intelligence organisation. Kell became a special constable and died on 27 March 1942.

Basil Thomson

Thomson's star was firmly in the ascendant in 1917. The return to Special Branch of duties connected with industrial disputes (following the dissolution of PMS 2, the Ministry of Munitions intelligence department), meant he had the ear of senior politicians frightened about revolution at home. In 1919 he became Home Office director of intelligence incorporating Special Branch within an organisation for domestic intelligence gathering. His natural right-wing inclinations meant he saw political events in the worst possible light, and it's safe to say he scare-mongered when reporting on left-wing movements. He exceeded his authority in using his uniformed officers without consulting the commissioner and had to be reminded that, in his police duties, he was a subordinate, and was instructed personally to submit a weekly report on the royal and ministerial protection duties being carried out, as well as all the other activities of the Special Branch officers. He proposed MI5 should be incorporated into one central intelligence organisation headed, naturally, by himself, and Kell was able to resist this only with the backing of the director of military intelligence. In 1921 Lloyd George 'retired' him summarily, without an official explanation, though the press speculated it was because of a security failure at Chequers. In 1922 Thomson wrote *Queer People* about his work in Special Branch, appearing to take the credit for the discovery, as well as the arrest and prosecution, of the spies captured during the war. This did not sit well with MI5.

On 12 December 1925, Thomson was arrested, along with a young lady, Thelma De Lava, for committing an act of indecency in Hyde Park (it was alleged she was 'manipulating his person'). Recognised by the sergeant at the police station, he appeared to give a false name (Hugh Thomson rather than Basil Thomson), and was directed to attend Marlborough Street Police Court on 14 December, which he failed to do. Miss De Lava also failed to attend. The commissioner advised the officers to proceed as they would usually. De Lava was traced and charged. She pleaded guilty and was fined £2. At his trial, Thomson argued he had gone to the park to research a new book on solicitation and explained that at the police station he had given his name as Home (pronounced Hume) Thomson, using his middle name. The latter story was accepted, but he was found guilty of the indecency offence and fined £5. He immediately appealed, and at the hearing Thelma De Lava gave evidence against him. Despite attempts to discredit police evidence and the presence of a number of prominent character witnesses, the appeal was dismissed.

Thomson spent much of the rest of the 1920s and 1930s in France, and continued to write both novels and books about the police and the war. He died on 26 March 1939.

Robert Nathan

During 1915 Nathan was gradually shifted to work involving Indian seditionist groups. Through the Censorship Department he discovered an Indian seditionist and Italian anarchist plot, hatched in Switzerland and financed in Germany, for (allegedly) the assassination of every one of the heads of the Allied nations, which resulted in details being leaked to the Swiss police and the plot thwarted. In 1916 he went to the USA and helped the US authorities in the smashing of German plots with Dr Chandra Chakravarti to supply weapons to a planned revolt in India, leading to the successful 1917/18 conspiracy trials in San Francisco.

In 1919 he was a key player in Foreign Office talks with Maxim Litvinov in Scandinavia about the release of British subjects still held in Russia. Though the mission was headed by a Labour MP (Mr O'Grady), Nathan and Lionel Gall (an SIS officer) seem to have done much of the negotiating. He was later proposed to head the British trade mission to Moscow (actually a cover for SIS operations), but ill-health prevented him from taking up the post. He died in 1921.

Ernest Anson

Anson remained with G Branch until 31 December 1919. He worked closely with SIS officer Redmond Burton Cafferata in the running of double agents in Switzerland in 1917, with Cafferata running the agents on the ground and Anson co-ordinating things from London. During the 1920s and 1930s he served in the Public Security Department, Ministry of the Interior, Cairo, monitoring Bolshevik activity in Egypt and Palestine. He was awarded the Insignia of Officer of the Order of the Nile, 1938 'in recognition of valuable services rendered by him in the employment of the Egyptian Government'.

John Fillis Carre Carter

Carter remained as head of G Branch until March 1918, when he transferred to the Intelligence Mission in Rome, which liaised closely with Italian intelligence. He left Rome in February 1919 and joined the Metropolitan Police where he was deputy assistant commissioner, in charge of Special Branch 1922–38, and assistant commissioner, Metropolitan Police, 1938–40. He resigned in September 1940. It's likely that Carter was the policeman whose application for the post of chief of the Secret Intelligence Service in late 1939 caused the three armed services to settle their differences and agree to the appointment of the soldier, Stewart Menzies, to the post. Carter died on 14 July 1944.

Henry Honywood Curtis-Bennett

Curtis-Bennett left MI5 in October 1917 to become an assistant to Basil Thomson at Scotland Yard, but remained an RNVR officer until he was demobilised in February 1919, when he returned to his legal practice. He was elected Conservative MP for Chelmsford in 1924 and served until 1926. He defended some of the most high-profile cases of the day, including Herbert Armstrong, the Hay solicitor accused of poisoning his wife (1922); Ronald True, the drug taking murderer (1922); and Sir Almeric Fitzroy, on charges of annoying women in Hyde Park (1922). He was defending barrister in the Irish sedition trial of 1923, and in 1929 he defended 'Colonel Barker', a woman charged with having married another woman whilst disguised as a man. When Basil Thomson was charged with the indecency offence in Hyde Park in 1925, Curtis-Bennett appeared for him. In 1933 he defended former SIS officer Compton Mackenzie at his Official Secrets Act trial.

He died on 2 November 1936 aged 57, dropping dead immediately after finishing a speech at the Dorchester. Basil Thomson wrote of him:

> As one who worked closely with Sir Henry Curtis Bennett throughout the war, I can testify to his great gifts as an examiner of suspects. He sat with me at Scotland Yard practically throughout the war, and almost all the suspects taken off ships or travelling through England came before us. It was interesting to note that when he was most dangerous to the guilty was when his manner was most suave and gentle. I came to know those danger signals when I turned an examination over to him. He was a delightful colleague to work with, and had a quiet humour about him that was most refreshing.

Charles Clive Bigham

Bigham remained with the Paris Intelligence Mission until 1919 when, after the Treaty of Versailles, 'Our archives had to be gone through in detail before they could be sent out to a huge incinerator in the fortifications and burnt; and then I handed over what remained of my business to the Military Attaché and to the War Office.' In 1929 his father died and he became a member of the House of Lords and, in 1945, Liberal chief whip in the House. He sat on numerous public bodies and wrote several books, including a two-volume autobiography *A Picture of Life* and *Journal and Memories*. He died in 1956.

Madame Gompertz

Whatever the exact nature of Mr and Mrs Gompertz's non-return visa, it obviously didn't apply after the war because by 1921 they were back in London. Leopold died on 26 January 1922, resident at 15 Warwick Square, London. Henriette was his executor and he left an estate worth £728 10s 10d. She returned to Holland and died there in 1940.

Frederic Decseny

In March 1941 Decseny, described as a former Bucharest correspondent of the *Detroit Free Press* and the London *Daily Mail*, was among the prisoners held by the Vichy regime in a prison camp for aliens at Le Vernet, where he had been sent without charge or trial. By 1944 he was back in Paris, living in the 10th District, when he was rounded up and sent to Auschwitz in convoy number 76 out of Drancy on 30 June 1944.

SOURCES

Two key sources, which do not appear to have been examined by other authors, are De László's Home Office Naturalisation file, which is at The National Archives (TNA) under reference HO 144/4238, and the Treasury Solicitor's file, also at TNA under reference TS 27/69, 'Philip Alexius Lászlós de Lombos: proposed denaturalization'. These files have not been digitised so a visit to TNA at Kew will be necessary to examine them. They are thick and the contents are frequently duplicated, but they present the basics of the case against the artist. Between them they contain enough correspondence from MI5 to enable a reconstruction of the basics of their investigation to be made.

There are other reports and correspondence relating to De László scattered throughout TNA's Foreign Office files for the period. FO 372/1027 contains, in file 192024, a brief report of a conversation between the Dutch ambassador and Lord Hardinge, permanent under-secretary at the Foreign Office, on abuse by De László of the diplomatic bag. FO 372/1109 and FO 372/1217 contain 1919 correspondence relating to attempts to obtain originals of De László's correspondence from abroad. FO 372/1257 discusses whether the case justified demanding the recall of the Dutch ambassador.

Portrait of a Painter: The Authorized Life of Philip de László by Owen Rutter, which was written with De László's help, was published in 1939 (Hodder and Stoughton) and paints a picture of a charming, intelligent, romantic and gifted man, one who made friends easily and stuck by them. Only occasionally, in De László's quoted notes and reminiscences, does a rather less pleasant man slip through, though some of this is almost certainly just as a result of our changed attitudes towards class and authority.

A more recent biography, as seen from his personal papers at least, *Philip de László: His Life and Art* by Duff Hart-Davis, in collaboration with Caroline Corbeau-Parsons (Yale University Press, London, 2010), is invaluable.

The full transcript of De László's Denaturalisation Committee hearing is in his Home Office naturalisation file (HO 144/4238), but it was extensively covered in the national and local press, much of which is now online. There is a more general file on the work of the committee at TNA in HO 144/13376 Certificates of Naturalisation (Revocation) Committee: appointment, duties, interim reports, general report, list of cases, etc.

Full texts of both the Defence of the Realm Act (DORA) and the Aliens Restriction Act can be found online using the *London Gazette* website.

MI5 files that have been made public are available at TNA in their KV series. On MI5 staffing levels, methods and

procedures, KV 1 series is invaluable, though there is nothing specific on the De László case. The whole KV 1 series
can be downloaded, free, from TNA website via their digital
microfilm service at http://nationalarchives.gov.uk/records/
digital-microfilm.htm. *The MI5 Game Book* (based on the
record books held by large estates of animals shot hunting)
is in KV 4/112 – KV 4/114, providing figures and case histories of men and women convicted of espionage, but it doesn't
include details of those, like De László, who were interned by
committee on MI5's advice.

There are two reports, written in 1919 by Booth, Brodie and
(presumably) Fetherston in KV 4/16 at TNA, which give some
details of the Special Section and its work, though it doesn't
(unfortunately) give any details on their secret methods.

There are interesting and extensive reports on cable censorship and postal censorship at TNA in DEFE 1/130 and DEFE
1/131. They give histories of the sections involved, the legal
framework behind them, methods, information that was gathered and what it was used for. Both mention the De László case.

Censorship Department reports are scattered throughout the
Foreign Office files, but the reports quoted revealing the par-
lous state of the Austrian population in 1916 come from FO
382/1140, FO 371/2862 and FO 382/1767 among others.

For a general history of MI5 during the First World War,
the official history *The Defence of the Realm: The Authorised
History of MI5* by Christopher Andrew (Penguin Books, 2010)
is a valuable starting point, though it makes no mention at all
of the László case.

The War Office doesn't seem to have released its copies of MT1(b)'s intelligence reports but, fortunately, copies sent to the Royal Flying Corps (part of the army at the time) were later passed to the Royal Air Force who have released them. AIR 1/550/16/15/27 – *Home Defence Intelligence Summaries: Aliens, etc* – contains these reports for late 1914 and early 1915, from which many of the cases mentioned in Chapter 1 are derived.

There are references to the espionage work of the Austrian Consulate in Berne in *The First World War: Germany and Austria-Hungary 1914–1918* by Holger H. Herwig in the Bloomsbury Modern Wars series and *The First World War: And the End of the Habsburg Monarchy, 1914–1918* by Manfried Rauchensteiner, as well as in an article 'The Regi Carabinieri: Counterintelligence in the Great War' by Alessandro Massignani (*Journal of Intelligence History*, Winter, 2001).

Basil Thomson's indecency trial was widely covered in the press and the Metropolitan Police file on the case is at TNA in MEPO 10/10. Basic details of his career have been derived from *Who's Who*, as have details of several of the other more prominent persons referred to in the book, and there are files on Thomson in HO 144/21176, HO 144/1590/380368 and HO 286/136, which provide more information. Though most files created by Special Branch (in MEPO 38 series) are retained, large numbers of reports are scattered throughout HO and FO series but require a lot of work to locate.

Private and Official by Nourah Waterhouse and Ronald Dockray Waterhouse (J. Cape, 1942) contains two stories relating to her late husband's time with MI5, which appear to suggest that the service was interested in breaking into diplomatic bags during the First World War.

King's Counsel: The Life of Sir Henry Curtis-Bennett by Roland Wild and Derek Curtis-Bennett (MacMillan, New York, 1938) has some interesting stories of his time with MI5 and details of his more unusual later cases. It also backs up one of Nourah Waterhouse's stories about breaking into a diplomatic bag.

MI6 and the Machinery of Spying (Philip H.J. Davies, Frank Cass, 2004) is invaluable in understanding the organisation of SIS and in particular giving information on N Section.

Though relating only to the Second World War, TNA file FO 1093/143 contains plenty of evidence of the extensive breaking into neutral diplomatic bags during that war.

Details of the Italian secret service break-in at the Austrian Consulate in Zurich are contained in a report within the Templeton Papers in Cambridge University Library.

Maundy Gregory's War Office file, mentioning his early secret work for the authorities and containing his rejected application to join the intelligence services, is at TNA in WO 339/124709.

The War Office file on Harold Spencer, the man whose bizarre allegations prompted the Pemberton Billing libel case and which details some of his own peculiar habits, is in WO 339/41960.

There are papers on the von Horst case at The National Archives in FO 383/143 file, FO 383/144 and CAB 24/4, and there's a masterful exposition of the case in Thomas Boghardt's 'A German Spy? New Evidence on Baron Loius von Horst' which appeared in *The Journal of Intelligence History 1* (Winter, 2001).

Spies of the Kaiser: Plotting the Downfall of England, probably the most famous of William Le Queux's collections of spy tales, was republished in 1996 by Frank Cass & Co. Ltd and has an excellent introduction by that master debunker, Nicholas Hiley.

Spies of the Kaiser: German Covert Operations in Great Britain During the First World War Era by Thomas Boghardt (Palgrave MacMillan, 2004) is a much more sober and well-researched examination of the realities of the situation based on German records. It also touches briefly on the von Horst case.

Intelligence and Imperial Defence: British Intelligence and the Defence of the Indian Empire 1904–1924 by Richard J. Popplewell (Frank Cass, 1995) is invaluable on the early career of MI5 official Robert Nathan and on the reach of British intelligence globally. It also mentions the use of a successful double agent, Victor Krafft.

Queer People by Basil Thomson (Hodder & Stoughton, 1922) is available free online via the Canadian National Library at https://archive.org/stream/queerpeople00thomuoft#page/n0/mode/2up.

My own book *Tracing Your Secret Service Ancestors* (Pen and Sword, 2009) contains lots of information about the early days of MI5 and how to research individuals connected with both it and Special Branch.

INDEX